THE WAY IT IS

R PRESTON TODD

BALBOA.
PRESS

A DIVISION OF HAY HOUSE

Balboa Press books may be ordered through booksellers or by contacting:

Balboa Press
A Division of Hay House
1663 Liberty Drive
Bloomington, IN 47403
www.balboapress.com
1 (877) 407-4847

Print information available on the last page.

ISBN: 978-1-5043-5480-6 (sc)
ISBN: 978-1-5043-5481-3 (e)

Balboa Press rev. date: 09/02/2016

Prologue

It is quiet. There is nothing *but* infinity and silence. Then, an instant later it is still quiet, but there are now three simple pieces defining existence by their capacity to accommodate everything. An instant later, there is a *Big Bang* and it is quiet no longer.

Descriptive terms are assigned to these three pieces, in order they not be confused with the multitudes of explanations that have come along since under other labels: the *Infinite*, the *Finite*, and the *Power of Creation*.

The *Infinite* must include everything as well as the other pieces (as per theories of infinity), but for the purposes of this discussion, it is everything that is invisible and non-physical. There is no place it is not. The *Finite* is effectively the opposite: visible and physical. The *Power of Creation* is the process by which stuff becomes stuff, i.e. moving from invisible to visible, non-physical to physical, and back again. This process is a function of perception itself.

Once things are physical, they get manipulated. Before science, this was totally in the realm of religion, trying to turn water into wine. *Let me know when that happens – I'm dying for a box of water!* In science, some branches investigate the *Power of Creation*, but perception is still a function of consciousness.

You have probably read multitudes of other books in the spirituality realm. Or maybe you're a newbie ... so this book will be read from the experienced to the novice. In either case there is a Glossary for terms which might be used differently than you are used to.

From works by Deepak Chopra to **The Course in Miracles**, many have been read, sometimes many times over, studied, and then merged into my existence. And there are many more where they came from. Previously they were books of the "dead tree" variety – now eBooks can be re-read on Kindle as desired, as well as doing a bunch of other things, like search, highlight, copy / paste into other documents, etc.

Kindle boasted its ability to hold 3,000 books, and would be easy to fill it up with nothing *but* spiritual works. More than one cross-referenced copy of the *Bible*, as well as multiple versions of *The Course in Miracles* would probably fill it all by themselves! After all, look at the size of the *Bible*. Speaking of "dead tree" books, they even print the *Bible* and *The Course in Miracles* on *extra thin* paper. In digital form, they take up a lot of bits-and-bytes!

Upon acquiring my first music CD, I swore to never replace any analog vinyl with digital, but ultimately decided differently. A similar mistake with "dead tree" vs. digital eBooks was never made. Especially after burning *(kidding)* or giving away my paper books, the Kindle provides for reading it again, or any of the other things including search one or all books, *plus Kindle books do not take up all that shelf space!* All you have to do is download it.

In *The Way It Is*, items looked at differently than usual, or brand new, are:

- The evolution of consciousness
- The three pieces of existence are given new labels
- Programming and re-programming the brain
- Stories, as given by "Organized Religion"
- The Roadmap-of-Life analogy aka the Akashic Records
- $E = mc^2$ ... Einstein got it almost right
- Affirmations and Meditation also fit with reality
- Emotions and Creativity have no words attached
- The ego *cannot* be used to provide brand new solutions
- Some thoughts about infinity
- You *can* turn your ideas into reality

You will find humorous comments here-and-there to keep anyone with a sense-of-humor engaged (sorry if you don't have one!) The humor is highlighted in this manner to help you differentiate fact from fiction.

Similarly, words and apropos definitions are added to a Glossary at the end for those not familiar with them, or how they are used here. My own personal spiritual evolution is briefly touched upon bringing me to this point. Consciousness is indeed evolving … witness what you are reading!

You will encounter subjects and terms repeated from different vantage points, in order you "get" what is portrayed. Not assuming anyone is too dense to "get it," but rather to make or emphasize a point. Besides, a whole lot of material is covered. By reading this, you will not only "get it," but thoroughly at that! You will find some new angles on familiar subjects you probably never thought about.

The verdict is largely in – physical evolution occurred over a long time, from chemicals to single-cell organisms that ultimately became plants or animals. The big "butt" *(as in Plumber's Crack)* is why everyone seems to consider evolution to include everything "living," but largely excludes non-physical consciousness. Why is our focus on physical evolution, while ignoring the possibility of the evolution of consciousness we are in *by definition*? Could it be the dominance of science … *or maybe Plumbers?*

Most spiritual books deal with only one fairly narrow topic, and how you could use that specific topic to change an area of your life for the better. It is usually given with detailed instructions, and as such are like cookbooks or diets. Here you will find a broader perspective, related to how your reality is actually created, given how the Universe works. You can use this book as a "how-to" guide to improve your life in general, but that is not the intention.

The intention is to present a different slant from other books you may have read, and assume evolution occurs not only physically, but in consciousness as well. Our physical body is complex, so who's to say our consciousness does not exceed it, since it preceded it? Complexity may be why the evolution of consciousness has not been popularly addressed.

This evolution of consciousness is evidenced by changes in various religions as they have come along, with science coming in recently; they both morphed into areas containing aspects of both called *New Thought*, *Quantum Physics*, and the *Law of Attraction*.

The questions regarding YOUR reality needing an answer are: what do you see when you open your eyes in the morning and climb out of bed, and how did it get there? But the most important question is: how can you effect your reality, presumably for the better?

This is one of the purposes of religions through the ages: to answer these questions. How religions answered these questions is open for interpretation, especially with all the other factors mixed in. The intention of this book is to answer the simple, yet specific, questions just asked. If answers to other questions you've had all along also arrive, that's good too!

Besides attempting to understand how things become "real," the older or more organized religions added morality and other community-building aspects into the mix. Religion was the "one-stop-shop" for a "governable" community. Remember, religion preceded government long before European rulers claimed to be directly descended from Jesus – *however that was supposed to have happened.*

But government is not our concern here – going from the invisible to the visible is. Then what about the physical results? After it's all said-and-done, going from the *Infinite* (a possibility) to *Finite* (reality) is what it's all about, then manipulating the results. This has been driving religion *and* science through the years.

There has been an effort, as long as time has been around, to "understand" how things get from the invisible to the visible. Some will attach the label of "spirituality" to this effort; others have other labels, sometimes of "religious" origin. It doesn't matter what label you attach, the effort is the same. But there is one shortfall – understanding something only applies to reason, which applies mostly to the *Finite* side of creation.

Of course, reality can *only* be right here, right now, in the present. Do you have reality tomorrow or yesterday? Your memories of yesterday, or your plans for tomorrow are *not* reality. You *will* have a reality tomorrow, as tomorrow turns into today and continually turns into the present. But soon enough, tomorrow is today is yesterday. Gone, except in memory.

Right here and right now is the *only* reality anyone ever has, and the *only* time-frame in which you can take action. Try taking action yesterday or tomorrow. *Planning* to take action tomorrow does not count! You must actually *take* action. But there are actions you can take *right now* to effect your reality tomorrow, as tomorrow turns into today, before it's just a memory.

Obviously, the afterlife as espoused by some religions does not apply to the here-and-now, but some interpretations of the soul might. Also, by concentrating on the here-and-*right*-now in the wrong manner, you might miss some aspects of how to *effect* your reality *tomorrow* and into the future, which will become your reality in the here-and-now quickly enough.

If you're still stuck on the five-thousand year, or seven-day "story," as well as "heaven" and "hell," first open your mind to the possibility these may be religious stories told before the current era of science and reasoning came along. Religious stories will be discussed in this light, and you can take away some profundities in-keeping with today's often secular world. Words are discussed, especially since stories use words.

Religion was once the complete domain of mystics like Popes, Saints, and other gurus. They had un-measurable things like faith and prayer in their toolbox, and nothing could be predicted. *Although your after-life was predicted. You would go to Heaven if you prayed regularly and followed the Ten Commandments (and tithed), or else you would be pushing the down-button in the afterlife elevator. How can you measure or predict somebody's ability to walk on water anyway?*

Then science came along, under the domain of scientists. Everything was measurable, there were equations for everything, it was predictable, and what wasn't already known was shortly to have its own equation. Religion was given the boot by left-brainers in the age of secularity, but the pendulum swings both ways.

Science used to be completely in the rational realm of the physical. Researchers are busy "proving" the accuracy of oral traditions (stories) handed down before printing, to say nothing about proving religion. Once in the domain of the physical, science now has a branch called Quantum Physics where the un-measurable right-brain relationship to the physical is intimately involved … the Law of Attraction is also under study by physicists.

We are in the evolution of un-measurable consciousness (religion) and the measurable physical (science), regardless. The pendulum swings more one way than the other at different times, regardless of those with a vested interest in keeping them separate. In the unified whole to which the pendulum is attached, right-brain (religion) to left-brain (science) is now swinging back to the middle in the evolution of consciousness.

What you see when you open your eyes every day is your own personal version of reality. The process of moving from the invisible to the visible many call "life." Among other things, to keep things from getting confused whereby there is obviously life, and then apparently not, but it "comes back" (as in a perennial plant), the term the *Power of Creation* is often used.

The *Infinite* filters down through invisible (shared) mass consciousness of different forms, has energy merged with, applied to, and changed by it. It ultimately becomes your very own personal and complete representation of what is going on in your brain, for you to see and experience as reality. What you see is uniquely yours; it comes only from yourself. Does what you see come from someone else? *How does that work? The last time I looked, it was me doing the looking!*

The challenge of where reality comes from to the *(air quotes)* "non-believer" then becomes to provide a dividing line: this comes from me and my decisions, and this doesn't. Where would the line be? Latching onto global events, you will say "A-HA! I didn't do *that!*" But you *did* choose to be *aware* of <whatever-it-is>, and so cannot claim complete innocence.

Others are completely unaware of that particular circumstance, and are not bothered in the least by what they're not aware of. "But they're ignorant!" you say. *Put on a black robe and be a judge!* And so you *choose* to be what you would call "informed." It is your individual choice, to know or not to know, so the question remains regarding where the dividing line is.

Sometimes when turning on the TV, the part of the NEWS is on about: how many people were shot last night; how many car crashes there were; how many home invasions; how many people died in house fires; *and yada-yada-yada.* "Now *that's* what I really needed to know!" and can do so much about, especially since it was last night … and the channel gets quickly turned. *I choose to be ignorant about such matters. But don't judge me!*

To the extent you hold anyone or anything else responsible for a part of your life, to that extent you are a victim and have surrendered your power. You got right where you are as the end result of all the choices you have made in your life especially assuming you are an adult – *and yes, it IS easier to blame someone or something else!*

There are those comfortable in their un-comfortability, who think they are personally responsible for *nothing*, so they live their lives as a complete victim. Everything happens *to* them, and they faithfully watch the NEWS and read the paper to stay informed. They do their best to cope and remain happily unhappy because there's nothing they can do about it – they think. It's like turning on the NEWS to see how many people died in house fires last night. There's nothing you can do about it, except choose *not* to watch. *Don't tell anyone you are thereby effecting your reality. There will be a test for the fully informed to see if you can remember how many people were killed last night!*

There is an entire system of manifestation based on an ancient Hawaiian tradition (that itself came from elsewhere, and may pre-date "Western" religion) called ho'oponopono in which the practitioner claims complete responsibility for *everything* in their life. They then proceed with a cleaning and erasing process to rid themselves of beliefs that might even come from *outside* themselves (or from historical memories) that were in error. [1]

There are three states any person might be living in:

1) Victimhood – where things "happen" to you. The vast majority of people live their entire lives in this state. Of course, there is no stopping other states from briefly occurring, but most existing in the victim state would just deny or ignore them.

---

[1] Vitale, Joe; Len, Ihaleakala Hew (2009-05-18). Zero Limits: The Secret Hawaiian System for Wealth, Health, Peace, and More (all pages). Wiley. Kindle Edition.

2) Self-Empowerment – this state might be best characterized by the individual employing methods like affirmations and meditation. They would probably "slide backwards" into the victim state often, and would catch an occasional glimpse of the inspired state if they are so inclined.

3) Inspired – this is where a person gets spirit guidance (aka Inspiration) from the "zero state" as described in the *Zero Limits* book, or "the Void" in Zen. This state is called the *Infinite* (while infinity itself is often called "Zero.")

If one were to draw a line representing the continuum of the above states, with Victimhood at one end and Inspired at the other (with Self-Empowerment in the middle), the book you are reading would fall into the Self-Empowerment "zone" leaning heavily toward the Inspired end. As in everything else, other philosophies would break the states down differently.

If one is interested, *and ready*, to read and learn more about what living an inspired life might look like, one source would be *Zero Limits*. As always, there are many other sources and workshops, etc. available regarding living an inspired life.

There are those living in the victim state who are held in awe by others also living as a victim. Those held in awe are perceived to be "better off, have it all" … except for the things the viewing public cannot see. The "better off" may drive a Beamer and live in a McMansion with a three-car garage, but are buried under mountains of debt, their health is failing, as well as their marriage. They are busy "keeping up with the Joneses!"

The better off give fodder for *Oprah*. If it gets bad enough, the better off person could be on *The Dr. Phil show*: "How's that workin' out for ya … now?" If life gets really, really bad, the better off person can be on *The Jerry Springer show*, where Jerry springs *(how apropos can you get?)* cat-clawing wives, ex-wives, and lovers on each other. *Better to stay fully informed by watching these shows as well as watch the NEWS and read the paper!*

"At least I didn't do *that*!" you might exclaim, after watching yet another screaming ex-wife coming out from behind the curtain. But the person watching ***The Jerry Springer show*** chose to watch it … whose decision is it to watch ***The Jerry Springer show*** anyway? Again: where *is* the dividing line between you are creating your own reality, and had nothing to do with it?

One might say there are other factors involved like mass consciousness, or politics. But you are subject to them only as you choose to be subject to them. There is a mass reality called time, aka linear time, but there are many methods to step outside of it. For instance, when you open your mouth to speak, do you know how the sentence ends? Co-incidences also step outside of time … can you predict when they will occur? There's also a mass reality called gravity, and I understand there are some who levitate. Like they say, "I'll believe it when I see it!" Perhaps a better permutation would be the reverse: "I'll see it when I believe it!" *It's like Deja-vu all over again!*

Politics is, well, politics: the job of giving stuff away that somebody else worked for, as well as telling everyone else what to do or not do (and how). In 10, 100, 1,000 years or at some "future" time people will say "What were they thinking?" Some future Dr. Phil will say "how's politics been workin' out for ya?" Many victims assume politics *is* their own reality, as they continue to watch the NEWS, read the paper, and vote.

We are seemingly much too slow evolving from Kings and Queens, and tin-pot dictators exist elsewhere on the globe. TV and newspapers, and whatever else someone thinks is worthwhile to serve up to us as NEWS still exist. If you still watch, listen, and read something you can do nothing about, thereby affecting your consciousness and your future reality, your choice is your choice. "How's that workin' out for ya?"

People like to tell everyone else what to do, which may have come from a childhood being subject to a sibling emulating a parent. You would hope the directions they give at least worked for the person espousing them. If you think there are a lot of exercise, diet and *(incongruously)* cookbooks out there, try spirituality. Try looking into religious works to tell you how to live your life – there are many different variations. These include different versions of the ***Bible***, which take translating, interpreting, and church classes to even *attempt* to understand! Telling everybody else what to do is so much easier than actually doing it yourself. Doing things other people tell you to do is easy!

An extra bennie: one can make a whole lot of money telling others what to do – note the televangelist who was going to push the big DOWN button in his spiritual elevator if he didn't get one million dollars. In today's world, there are many who call themselves "coaches" or "politicians" who make a good living telling others what to do or not do, and how. Some have done absolutely nothing in their lives other than tell everybody else what to do. *The worst are the ones that have royally screwed-up everything they ever tried to do, but are now telling everybody else what to do and how to do it. Plus they have copped a better-than-you 'tude!*

If there is one solution that works, everybody would be doing it already. Note a standard tip: "Buy Low, Sell High." So why isn't everybody doing *that* already? Maybe because a variation on the theme makes just as much sense: "Buy High, Sell Higher." So if these things make so much sense, why are people buying high and selling low? Could it be whatever pack mentality has everyone following the other lemmings off the cliff? *A good philosophy might be: "When you find the person who will never die, I'll do what they're doing!"*

Such reasoning concerning following someone else's advice comes from the ego, whose job it is to protect us. The ego seems to like being told what to do, and there *is* safety in numbers. If everyone else is doing it, it can't be all *that* bad, can it? Hint: YES. *Remember what your Mother said about everyone else jumping off a bridge? How about when everybody is buying – there was a dot-com craze and don't forget Tulip bulbs.*

There was a popular principle known as much for its acronym as its substance: "KISS" standing for "Keep It Simple Stupid." So another intention for this book is: to boil down *(a cookbook reference!)* all the material into something indeed simple ... well, as simple as can be, given the eons of explanations and directions. *That's another reason to use different terms.*

You can't pull something out of a bag that was not there all along. We came into this reality under the rules governing it which were always there. What you see is uniquely yours, and can come only from yourself. It was there all along!

Preface

There was a PBS telethon featuring Deepak Chopra, MD on the TV. For those not aware of him, he gives a very straight-forward view of Universal Unity and how science and spirituality are coming together, after having served in both areas.

This particular PBS special was titled ***The Future of God***. In the title there's "[the big G-Man]" *(and I mean "big G" literally, as in uppercase "G")*. Since many don't like the "G" word, attempts to delete references to God farther on are made by substituting "[the big G-Man]" for the "G" word. But it *is* in the title of the Chopra work, and I downloaded it onto Kindle. *So sue me.*

All lawyers reading this far have perked up their ears, being involved in a vocation where no-one is actually responsible for anything! Shakespeare gave us the famous line paraphrased here: "First kill all the lawyers."

There was an original Star Trek episode where they did so, and it didn't work out well. That particular show must have been written by an attorney (notice how they never call themselves lawyers)!

Also notice how phonetically similar "lawyer" and "liar" are. What did the actor say in the Western: "You callin' me a lawyer?"

Personal responsibility for your own life is a theme engaged with many times. Signing a contract drawn up by a qualified lawyer would seem to ensure personal responsibility. Until a presumably better lawyer is hired to find a way out. Shaking hands on an understanding would also seem to ensure personal responsibility, until the hand-shaker chooses to walk away. But "[the big G-dude]" is unlike any other lawyer regarding your life.

There is no contract to sign, nor can you walk away from life. You are responsible for yourself whether you like it or not. You can't find any lawyer to get you out of it, nor can you pay *(excuse me, donate)* enough to a Priest to annul your life. Priests (choose the title for your own religious "official") are like lawyers for the right-brain; lawyers use laws and contracts with words and are, well, lawyers for the left-brain. They are all there to interpret the "laws" governing the *Power of Creation. Plus they have that black robes thing going on.*

Like every other vocation, lawyer-ing has its good and bad practitioners – you just need to draw a line to distinguish between them. Like the line you would need to draw to determine what part of your life you are responsible for, and what part you aren't. *Everyone likes to be responsible for the good parts, and hold someone else responsible for the bad. Since they are already responsible for what many would term "bad," let's just blame lawyers. Or politicians, since most of them are lawyers-from-Hell anyway.*

Hopefully you choose a lawyer (or priest) from the good side of the line ... have fun choosing. Abraham Lincoln was a "good" lawyer, and a politician to boot! So somebody shot him. There are still some good lawyers, so killing them all seems an over-compensation. It probably wouldn't work out well ... *at least according to that Star Trek episode. But it's fun to think about! It would certainly solve the politician over-population problem in DC.*

Religions use their equivalent of lawyers, and actual lawyers have been around as long as there have been words in laws and contracts. Wouldn't it be nice if there were one firm that could represent *both* sides of your life? *The firm's shingle could read "Lawyers for Life," and all qualified employees could wear black robes and be judgmental, especially on Sunday.*

The coming back together of religion and science is a viewpoint espoused by *Religious Science*, and other *New Thought* philosophies. Hence the official name "Religious Science" tries to encapsulate the coming-together view by embracing both religion and science. Their other unofficial, possibly more popular name – "Science of Mind" – uses the religious aspect in the title by using "mind" along with "science," which is the title of their "textbook" written by the founder of this movement, Earnest Holmes: *The Science of Mind*.

Dr. Wayne Dyer stars in many PBS specials, and formerly spoke at many Religious Science and other New Thought Centers. He epitomizes both science and religion, having evolved from science (psychology) into religion and spirituality. He doesn't necessarily speak about the connection between them, but at one point he just couldn't do any more science; even though his books up to that time were very popular, and his publisher wanted more psychology books.

Many will remember Dr. Dyer from his first bestseller psychology book, *Erroneous Zones*. This was written when he was still in the scientific and psychological mode. He evolved into a more spiritual mind-centric approach, and delves deeply into historic religious and spiritual philosophy, and all his books and works remain popular. He has written, at this count, some forty-some-odd books, traversing the whole gamut from science to religion … the latter ones more representative of the religious and spiritual view.

There are many different authors, speakers, and learned practitioners (Bob Proctor, Joe Vitale, Joe Dispensa, Bruce Lipton, Lisa Nichols for instance, many of whom were featured in the movie *The Secret*), some who have come at the mind-body-spirit connection from different angles, ultimately going back to BOTH a religious *and* scientific connection. But they seem to fall short of defining reality itself.

What is reality anyway? When we open our eyes and look around, *that's* our very own unique individual reality. Yours might encompass screaming kids, driving them to school, going to your job, picking up the kids from daycare, coming home, feeding them and yourself, then falling asleep in front of the TV. Then doing it all over again tomorrow.

By and large, most tolerate reality and do their best to cope with it. They are victims of life, have no idea they can change it with their mind, but might consider doing so if it would only result in life being more tolerable … but *so much more* is possible.

Remember the joy you had as a young-un, waking up every day? Your imagination had you playing games and making up stories with *Matchbox* or *Hot Wheels* or other toy cars on make-believe roads on the bedspread or rug in your bedroom. How about playing house in Barbie's play-house, while cooking something in an easy-bake oven so you can have high-tea with the Queen? The power of imagination was learned amidst mother's yelling.

You may vaguely remember this level of joy, or at least some details, from viewing pictures from your childhood (if you're not too embarrassed) or some TV shows. But have you experienced the same level of imagination and pure joy *today* you had as a kid? Probably not.

Today adulthood provides screaming, screeching, and fighting kids, mini-vans, and the PTA. TV, movies, and video games become an easy babysitter. Somehow just DOing more than the other kid's parents, and HAVEing more than our neighbors, will make us happy … or happier, at least. *Maybe Oprah … or Dr. Phil… or Jerry Springer will have us on!*

Join the PTA. Film your little one in the school play – along with every other parent filming their kid from the audience. Look at a view of the audience from the stage! Watch the film once, forcing the kid to watch for a while, since he or she is probably not interested. It's not just a kid-parent thing. After all, the kid experienced the play first-hand. Someday the parent will make it into a video montage, hopefully before any of the other parents.

Parents DOing more than the other kid's parents are happy, or happier at least, for a while.

Live life vicariously through your kids. *At some point they will be living life through their kids, now your grand-kids. And you can give the grand-kids cola, candy, and ice-cream – wind 'em up and send 'em home to their parents (your kids). Didn't you always say to your kids "Someday I will get even with you" anyway? What goes around stays around.*

Wouldn't you like the tables to be turned? Not turned all the way around, like it would be if your kids were living their life with the same lack of vitality as you live yours, but instead *you* are living your life with the same excitement kids have while on-stage. Not simply filming them, but *being* them – more grown-up, of course!

If only you could create your reality with the same imagination you had driving your *Hot Wheels* into town for the first time, filling up at the gas station and also getting an oil change. How about serving tea and Éclairs *(naughty, naughty)* to the Queen while wearing your tiara. Wouldn't you also like to create your reality this way? Just imagine.

By the time you finish reading this, you will be more familiar with terms like *Infinite, Finite,* and the *Power of Creation,* to help take various explanations associated with more traditional terms through time – out. You will "understand" that there is an *Infinite,* as well as the visible results of an idea occurring in your *Finite* reality. Of course, there is life itself, referred to as the *Power of Creation.* You will also be more comfortable with terms like imagination and visualization … there is even a discussion about inventions.

You will find a Glossary section. It is there to assist anyone new to the subject, as well as certain terms with which you might not be familiar, especially in the context used. You may want to start by reviewing this Glossary, to see what concepts might be new, as well as differences in the meaning of certain terms you might be more traditionally familiar with.

There is an organized religion, aptly named "Religious Science," which is a meeting point between religion and science. Their preferred term for infinite intelligence is the "objective"; an individual experience of our reality comes from the "subjective." Hint: see the Glossary.

A word about terms and definitions. When there are different or conflicting definitions, the term is used in the context of the discussion. You will find many who will argue about what a specific term is all about, aka its definition. Some religions will fight-to-the-death over what is essentially the same thing – different word. *Go figure. It's like fighting over the word for water in different languages.* For those wishing to argue, first realize arguing is in your reality.

About terms and definitions: start with an Internet search. If you wish to research a term further, start with Wikipedia, then go to Amazon.com, or your local library to get reading material. The resources are too numerous to mention – there's lots! You will discover the same thing. *Save fighting-to-the-death until last.*

Did you know there was a war between the Spanish and Portuguese over Seagull (not Johnathon Livingstone) poop found on some cliffs on the West side of South America? Apparently bird-poop is rich in some fertilizer. So they fought-to-the-death in the Great Bird Poop War!

There have been many explanations for the *Infinite* and the *Finite*, as well as the process of ideas going between them, using other terms. Non-standard (but still descriptive) terminology wrings any meaning given via all the explanations throughout the ages out. Describing these three basic components again using different words should help. The process of going between the *Infinite* and the *Finite*, as well as manipulating the physical results, some will call "life," and is often called the *Power of Creation* here.

There is this "state" called the *Infinite* (unbounded consciousness), which contains all possibilities. You can use the terms "Cosmic Consciousness" or "Infinite Intelligence" if you prefer. They haven't been used-to-death yet. "[The big G-Man]" is not used because it freaks many out ... as well as it having been used, abused, and explained so many times . . .

The next "state" is called the *Finite*, and is the visible part of reality. Even if there's a large number of items, like grains-of-sand on all beaches in all oceans and in all deserts, assuming they're visible and could theoretically be counted, they are in the *Finite*. Same thing with Galaxies (to say nothing of Suns), leaves-on-trees, blades-of-grass, etc. A lot of these are shared by everyone in our reality. *I'm sure there are planets somewhere with grains of sand!*

Think about this: you can't DO anything to the *Infinite*. Like the commercial for soup says "It's (already) in there!" And since the contents of the *Finite* are pre-determined (by spiritual law) regarding the *Power of Creation* process, that leaves you with only one relatively minor aspect of the original three components you can do anything about: the first-person part of the *Power of Creation* (consciousness) unique to yourself.

Do not confuse this writing with instructions on *how* to do something, like a cookbook. It's not that specific. It is intended to explain how reality is created, and you can take or leave anything presented as instructions. You *will* find instructions, but you are free to ignore these (as always), and find a better way more suited to your particular circumstances. You will find footnotes and suggested readings and other resources to explore further.

Our very own reality, like it or not, is created at every given moment – hour by hour, minute by minute, second by second, and instant by instant. Our reality is a perfect reflection, like a mirror, of what is going on in our brain, along with all the programming, filters, and other mass consciousness. You will learn a lot about how the Universe works. You can't change the reflection by hammering on the mirror! *But you might succeed in breaking the mirror. Good luck (pun intended) with that!*

Like the Religious Science motto that has been repeated many times:

"Change your mind – change your life."

Left Brain versus Right Brain

Many have heard of distinctions between the different hemispheres of the brain: left-brain and right-brain. For right-handed people, the left-brain controls the right side of the body. It is also the rational / logical / intellectual side of the brain, houses the ego, and thinks in words. Likewise, the right-brain controls the left side of the body but contains a link to the infinite. Left-handed people are the opposite regarding what-does-what in the different hemispheres of their brain.

There was an actual brain connected to a spine some researcher brought out in a box. *The original owner wasn't needing it any more.* There was light between the two sides ... so they really are separate. *In actuality, left-handed people got smacked so hard when they were born it reversed their polarity. Or maybe they did not go to Catholic school long enough to get beat into right-handedness and have other devilish behavior beaten out of them.*

Much understanding of what-does-what in the brain came *before* MRIs could light up what section of the brain was in use, from incidents like somebody winding up with a railroad spike in their head. *I would'a thunk that would'a hurt! (Such is my contribution to redneck-ism.)* The spikee lived to tell about it, and could afterwards walk around without pain – *the brain feels no pain* – but just couldn't do something, hence the knowledge of what area does what in the brain evolved. *The spikee had custom baseball hats made.*

For instance, if a section of someone's brain was injured and they could no longer speak, the area of the brain controlling speech could be determined. Much the same type analysis would determine the area of the brain involved in senses such as seeing, hearing, taste, etc. as well as control over bodily functions. *Get your mind out of the gutter. "Bodily functions" refers to talking about*

1

moving your fingers or arm. Sometimes multiple areas of the brain and physical functions were involved – specialists-of-the-day figured out a lot over time. *A lot of railroad spikes were used, and the custom baseball hat industry flourished.*

Then along came EEG technology to measure the frequency output from someone's brain. MRIs identified and measured active brain areas, without all the physical trauma *(assuming it is traumatic to see a railroad spike sticking out of your head).* Quite literally, we may someday be able to measure the active part in someone's brain as they are communicating with the *Infinite.* People are constantly looking at the brain with new techniques and instrumentation.

Getting the left and right halves of your brain to have the same measurable frequency (vibrate at the same rate) seems an admirable cause. Such is one of the stated objectives of **Transcendental Meditation**, often known as **TM**, and they show graphs to that effect. There is a scientifically validated factor known as "The Maharishi Effect" (Maharishi is the founder of TM) that states that a group focusing on a single cause achieves measurable effects. *Apparently focusing on world peace by Miss America contestants has not yet worked.*

Practitioners of TM demonstrate proof, through graphs of brain wave frequency scans, that brain synchronization (right to left side) is accomplished through this discipline. They also hypothesize a "critical mass" of people practicing this discipline can be demonstrated to change an entire section of a city, country or the world, with "proof" supplied in a scientific manner. Such an area would have less crime, or more peace-of-mind, according to what the Maharishi Effect predicts. All of these are worthwhile endeavors, *as would be world peace. Maybe Miss America contestants need to learn TM.*

TM was at least partially responsible for keeping my head from exploding in a turbulent time long ago. If this was the only benefit, it was well worth it. The supposedly secret and unique-per-participant mantra is still used occasionally in meditation. No comparison of mantras was made upon encountering others who also underwent TM training – it's the meditation that matters. *I have this feeling the mantras might all be the same! But that could just be the paranoid conspiracy theorist talking.*

From a larger perspective, even brains operating at the exact same frequency on both sides cannot unite both halves of the brain. Uniting reason and emotion is impossible; reason uses logic and words, while emotions use feelings and neither logic nor words. Maybe one side can support the other, and vice versa. This would presumably happen under the best possible conditions when both halves of the brain are operating around the same frequency – at least according to TM. Getting both halves of the brain to operate at similar frequencies might be a relatively minor issue. Getting left-to-right-brain *support* (and vice versa) might otherwise overshadow TM methodologies.

This would be a good place to mention some tools or techniques that help us use our inherent intuition, our right-brain link to the infinite. They are often known as "oracles" that "tap into" the knowledge of the Universe as it stands at that particular point in time.

The *I Ching* (pronounced E – long "E" – Ching) is an ancient Chinese guide using translations of 64 "hexigrams." A question is held in mind while 6 "throws" of devices used especially for this purpose are made. Results are noted as unbroken or divided lines, from the bottom up. Once complete, the corresponding hexagram is accessed, which contains the "answer" to the question asked. The answer is both general (like the astrology reading in the paper) but worded in such a way as to be unambiguous while indirect.

A pendulum is used to give "yes" or "no" answers to a question. The pendulum will yield either a "round-and-round" or a "straight line" "answer" which corresponds to "yes" or "no" ("true" or "false.") The subject will first set-up the session by asking a couple question with unambiguous and mutually exclusive answers, to determine which motion means "yes" and which means "no." He or she holds the static end of the pendulum against their "third eye" area on the forehead, and watches the pendulum movement. For instance (assuming one answer is "yes" or "true"), they might ask "Is my name Mary?" followed by "Is my name Fred?" while observing the pendulum movement. This will "calibrate" the pendulum.

Muscle testing usually requires an assistant. The subject holds his or her arms out to the side while making a statement. The assistant presses down lightly on the subjects arm. If the statement is true, the arm will hold steady, whereas if the statement is false, very little downward "pressure" will be required to collapse the arm. It is said the Universe will *not* support a falsehood, nor will your body support your outstretched arm. It can sometimes be done solo by holding a weight instead of having an assistant.

The "Magic 8-ball" is considered by some to be a toy, and so can be purchased in the toy-and-novelty section of some stores. It is used by posing a question while shaking or rotating the ball, until the time feels right to turn it over. It will read an unambiguous answer. When last unboxing one, a question was formulated … more-or-less. Upon turning it over for the answer, it read "Not Right Time." *Go figure.*

It has been said a deck of playing cards represents one of the most spiritual things in our reality, and so I held a statement in mind *with the corresponding feeling* while playing Solitaire on my computer. Against almost unimaginable odds (the ego and reason need to chime in!) results in *two succeeding games* were phenomenal, but I couldn't hold the feeling any longer after determining *something* was going on … but wasn't really testing it either. There could be no further duplication of results without engaging the "testing factor."

There was a method developed that could tell whether politicians are lying. But it always gave an affirmative response to the "are they lying now?" question, so politicians disavowed its use.

These are only some of the methods that are used to tap directly into the knowledge of the Universe. It is important to note, the results are at that particular point in time, especially when one is in a linear-time-frame reality. These can be modified, or added to, as valid changes or other methods become known. A word of caution about testing them is in order: testing the method would introduce an element of disbelief that effectively cancels the results (i.e. the "testing factor"). Use it when it feels right – not to test it. Do not use the oracle too often, or on inconsequential issues *as in what you should have for lunch today. Nothing is ever too easy, or everyone would know the techniques to make you rich playing the lottery!*

There are intuitive methods that are either more detailed and / or you must be aware of the intuition when it happens – you do not have any choice as to when. "Giving voice" to an intuition i.e. using words to term the intuition as "something" and writing it down, would be an activity that raised intuition to the level of your conscious awareness. [2]

Written follow-ups might include whether you took advantage of the intuition and if it worked, as well as actions taken. Writing is important, as it brings forth conscious left-brain awareness. Such, also, is the nature of journaling. Some suggest writing using the non-dominant hand to bypass the inherent logic and reasoning of the ego, *but try reading it later!*

These are given as exercises to begin waking up your intuition, and provide important written support to what would otherwise simply be gut feelings. Intuition uses spirituality to determine your

[2] Choquette, Sonia (2013-09-09). Tune In: Let Your Intuition Guide You to Fulfillment and Flow (all pages). Hay House, Inc. Kindle Edition.

future reality, and the rational brain supports the intuitive side with words – brain support in both directions.

What other right-brain activities might have the support of left-brain words and reasoning? The word "words" gives the first clue. What creative activity uses words? Journaling does, and you're reading words right now, so there's some clues.

There are many creative activities using words. Anything written, by definition, uses words. There's highly creative fiction versus less creative non-fiction, in book, article, short story, etc. format. While reading the words, excitement or fear might be "felt". Most movies use words as well as feelings, and there's also a written script or screenplay and possibly a preceding book. Then there's poetry, some so "intellectual" as to be non-understandable, resulting in feelings only. Journaling might enhance word-based (left-brain) knowledge. These are some examples where the logic normally inherent in words starts to merge with the creative half of the brain or the *Infinite*.

Even music is usually written. It uses the words of music: staff, notes, timing, etc. Musicians practice their trade using the language of music, then give a performance many interpret via emotion. Of course there's a song's lyrics (if it has them) … while writing them down, the words can be construed as also accessing the *Infinite*.

This would be a good place to interject another right-brain activity, sometimes supported by left-brain reasoning – faith. Definitions of faith tend toward: faith is a belief in things as yet unseen. Hence faith derives from the (as yet) invisible / non-physical. Religious Science uses the term "spiritual prototype," and Abraham often uses "spiritual escrow." [3]

---

[3] Hicks, Esther; Hicks, Jerry (2009-09-01). The Vortex: Where the Law of Attraction Assembles All Cooperative Relationships (all pages). Hay House. Kindle Edition.

Deepak Chopra gives a whole chapter about faith (both "good" and "bad") [4] as well as scripture offering more …

> *faith is the assurance of things hoped for, the*
> *conviction of things not seen [Heb 11:1]* [5]

Reasoning provides us with *persistence*, as well as telling us this is where the invisible changes into the visible. In Napoleon Hill's classic book Think and Grow Rich, an entire chapter is devoted to persistence. Hill said

> *"There may be no heroic connotation to the word*
> *'persistence,' but persistence is to character what*
> *carbon is to steel."* [6]

Carbon is added to iron to make steel. *There was an "iron age" but was there a "steel age?"*

There are many other creative activities not using words whatsoever. They cannot. Trying to explain a painting in words is like using words to explain how something smells or tastes. Try to explain what love or fear is, without quickly invoking the well-known circular definition of words. But we all know what they "feel" like. The Course in Miracles says:

> *You have but two emotions, and one you made and*
> *one was given you* [7]

---

[4] Chopra, Deepak (2014-11-11). The Future of God: A Practical Approach to Spirituality for Our Times (p. 58). Potter/TenSpeed/Harmony. Kindle Edition.
[5] Crossway Bibles (2011-02-09). The Holy Bible, English Standard Version (Kindle Location 47758). Good News Publishers/Crossway Books. Kindle Edition.
[6] Proctor, Bob (2015-06-09). The ABCs of Success: The Essential Principles from America's Greatest Prosperity Teacher (Kindle Locations 1402-1404). Penguin Publishing Group. Kindle Edition.
[7] Schucman, Helen (2011-05-06). A Course in Miracles: Original Edition (Kindle Locations 6485-6486). White Crow Books. Kindle Edition.

Try love out for a change – it might just be the emotion that was given you. All emotions would be variations on love or fear in this example.

The following is a halfway decent definition of what comes from the emotional side of the brain – it "feels" like something, regardless of whether you "made it up" or it was given. Sometimes feelings are *referred* to via words. Go ahead, try explaining in words what someone walking behind you down the street at night (fear) feels like to someone who has never had *any* experience of fear. *The fact it might be hard to find that person does not invalidate the point.* Logic cannot erase a feeling. You still feel fear no matter how "reasonably" safe and well-lit the street is. Have you ever "loved" someone for no "reason" whatsoever? Try to explain *that*! *(You cannot possibly say you like listening to the Love Song channel on AM radio if you're not "in love"!)*

Speaking again of the separate hemispheres of the brain, the left / reasoning side of the limited brain is literally opposite to, and separate from, the right / infinite half, which is in-turn linked to the power of the Universe with no words whatsoever in its vocabulary – only feelings. Never the twain shall meet, as they say … well, relatively never. Hint: Never say "never."

The "output" of the rational left-brain is words. The "output" of the emotional right-brain or creative side of the brain gives us "feelings" only alluded to via words. So while the left-brain reasoning-with-words side of the brain may never actually meet with the right-brain emotional-and-creative side, they do cooperate. And so continues the evolution of consciousness.

All that Stuff

You have had your hand stamped to enter the "Vast **Minority** Club" – your consciousness has caused you to be exposed to this knowledge. So why would anyone call a minority "vast?" Perhaps you might best understand by considering who is in the "vast **majority**."

The "vast majority" of people wake up every day at the *same* time, feed the kids at the *same* table, then go to their *same* place at the table to eat, shower in the *same* manner, drive down the *same* streets to take the kids to the *same* school, then go to the *same* job with the *same* boss and the *same* co-workers. Go to the *same* place for happy hour, then go home to eat, once again at the *same* place at the table, and get the kids to do their homework. Then watch the *same* shows on TV, put the kids down in bed at their time, go to bed at your time, and wake up *(via an alarm clock you do not even have to reset!)* the next day at the *same* time and do it all over again. Such is life for the "vast majority."

At best, breakfast, lunch, and dinner consist of different foods than yesterday, even if eaten at the *same* place at the *same* table. Then there's the weekend ... all different! Except it is mostly the *same* as other weekends. After all, you do have to cut the grass and weed the garden (the *same* as last week). Chances are good you take your two-week vacation at the *same* time-of-the-year, and go to the *same* place as last year. Such are the differences in life for the "vast majority."

People are lucky to not live in the time of the "vast" industrialization of that era, and are not screwing the *same* lug nut onto the *same* lug on the *same* wheel in the *same* manner all day every work day. Or sewing the *same* button onto the *same* shirt, in what became known as "sweat shops." Somebody "invented" air

9

conditioning in the interim, so the "sweat shops" that still exist in this country are not so sweaty.

In other areas in the globe making knock-offs, presumably you still sweat in a "sweat shop." Progress has assured people in *this* country are NOT *still sweating* over computers and robots because of the air-conditioning someone invented. *Do "boiler rooms" where you hear all the people talking in the background when you answer your phone count as "sweat shops?" Boilers are hot, right? But in India where those on help-lines speak better English than us, they have little AC … so by definition they are "sweat shops."*

Speaking of *same*ness … Henry Ford is quoted in Bob Proctor's (of **The Secret** fame) book **The ABCs of Success**:

> *"All FORDs are alike, all people are different."*

Further, Earl Nightingale said:

> *"The opposite of Courage is not Cowardice, it is Conformity."* [8]

If you work for the USPS, you still probably do the *same* thing all day every day, like in Henry Ford's day. If you are lucky enough to be able to get out and have a delivery route, you put the *same* stuff in the *same* mailboxes every day. One day a week there is the big newspaper flyer with all the store coupons. Basically the so called "mail carriers" are just overpaid glorified paper boys. *No wonder they "go postal!"* Alas, after a short period of excitement while going postal, if they are still alive they find life in prison is ever more of the *same*. Plus decisions for their own lives under their own personal responsibility has been taken away. They're not brave for going postal, they're cowards. Now they're in prison too. More of the *same*.

---

[8] Proctor, Bob (2015-06-09). The ABCs of Success: The Essential Principles from America's Greatest Prosperity Teacher (Kindle Locations 1097-1112). Penguin Publishing Group. Kindle Edition.

How many people are in this vast majority? Certainly more than 51% – maybe 70%, 90%, 95% or even 99.9% of the population. There is not an appropriate question on the Census, nor has a poll ever been taken. No-one knows what percentage of people are in the vast majority today. *But let's not give the Government any more ideas on how to spend our money on surveys, while making themselves feel useful. They're already busy figuring out how to pay for the USPS. GO Postal!*

For the vast majority of people on the incoming *and* outgoing side of the mailbox, life happens TO them, and they do their best to cope with mind-numbing *sameness. Like the bumper-sticker says: "Life's a Beach and Then You Die."* There is no conception you have any power over anything; you just cope with what comes along, and then you die.

What happened to the wonder of life you experienced as a child when you went to the beach with your red pail and yellow plastic shovel? Maybe you made sand castles, and imagined what castles were like in somebody's life. For the vast majority of people, imagination got removed by life *(or had it beaten out in Catholic school)*, so you're now ready to take your place in Corporate America not-so-sweaty sweatshops.

There are even bells signaling the beginning / end of class; afterward the next *same* class is shuffled to. K-12, Undergrad, graduate, post graduate, post-post graduate – they're all the *same.* In the sweatshop *(workplace)* the clock ticks inexorably toward 9:00 am or 5:00 pm. *They even have clocks that tick like those in elementary school! Rent* **Clock Watchers** *... the movie will remove you from reality for its running time.*

There's a reason they call it "happy hour." If you suck down enough half-price drinks while ogling your co-worker, you are happy for more than an hour! But if you're a member of the vast majority that has now climbed the corporate ladder to management, you may not be so "happy" any more in the same manner. Management does not degrade themselves by going to "happy hour," but they get more money, houses, jets, and yachts to be happy with … in or on their new toys. Now they're happy again for more than just one hour. Unless they married the co-worker they were ogling before, then they're not happy after she takes half the manager's stuff which presumably makes her and her well remunerated divorce lawyer happy.

Now the vast majority is understood, let's flip the "vast" coin over and consider the "vast minority." In reality, the two sides of the coin are not nearly the same size – such is the paradox of mind. Those left in the much smaller vast minority are the people knowing they *do* have control over their reality. Whether they live in conformity is by their own choice, and they accept only as much conformity as they want – but that person probably doesn't want conformity aka cowardice anyway. That's why they're in the vast minority.

So there it is, the difference: it's between the "vast majority" of people thinking one has *no control* over his or her environment, while the "vast minority" know they DO have control. If you have read this far, you are ready to sign up to take the prerequisite class to move from the vast majority and graduate into the vast minority. Just remember, reading a cookbook or taking a class on cooking does not make you a chef; in much the same manner understanding reality does not give you control over it, but at least it's a start. The bell has rung signaling the beginning of class, so shuffle onward.

We'll start with an easy question, one may think it is a bit trivial perhaps … but it is the opposite. What is the definition of "trivia" anyway? It would involve a "useless little bit of information." So the opposite of "useless" is "useful." And what would the opposite of a "little bit of information" be? Let's go as big as it gets – reality itself. So the opposite of "useless trivia" would be: "useful information covering reality itself."

You are now thinking the answer to the easy question might not be so easy after all. But it *is* easy, although certainly not trivial. All you have to do is look in the right places. A little question-hint most have heard before will make sure your thinking caps are all warmed up. The question is: "If a tree falls in the forest and no-one is around to hear it, does it still make a sound?" Think you know the answer? Read on ... and for the easy question itself.

The easy question cannot be answered right off, or people would find it, ponder it for a second or two, get their diploma (which allows them to think they are "enlightened"), and go on to the next chapter ... if at all. They are the ones who think if they just take enough classes and read enough, they will "get it." They will therefore have their enlightenment, and have enough diplomas to prove they "know it." They wallpaper their walls with diplomas as visible demonstrations of how they "get it" to everyone else, but chances are good they don't. *That's why they need diplomas all over their walls.*

Back to the tree-in-the-forest hint: "If a tree falls in the forest and no-one is around to hear it, does it still make a sound?" Assuming it "ripples the air" or whatever happens to make a sound someone perceives; if there are instruments around to measure the rippling, then presumably they would, but someone would have to read and interpret the results. Otherwise, who cares?

The correct answer would be: since sound is dependent on the observer, then if there is no observer, there is no sound. If you have another definition of sound, then have at it, but you would be *WRONG!* The left-brain ego separates us by making me *RIGHT* and you *WRONG!*

There is a TV show called ***The McLaughlin Group*** where the host seems to derive great pleasure by yelling at the panelists they are *WRONG.* Then McLaughlin proceeds to give the *RIGHT* answer – there are clearly defined rights and wrongs … via his left-brain ego anyway.

Saturday Night Live did great skits on that show. The McLaughlin character (Dana Carvey) asks the panelists to choose a number. After yelling at them they are *WRONG*, he proceeds to give the *RIGHT* answer. Maybe it was seven. McLaughlin was *RIGHT*, end everyone else is *WRONG*. But in the particular case of a tree falling in the forest, my ego tells me I AM *RIGHT*! It makes no sound unless someone is around to *hear* the sound. *There's also the sound of one hand clapping!*

A sound is, by definition, dependent on the observer; if there is no observer, then there is no sound! *There is either deductive or inductive logic in there, but I can never remember the difference. One form of logic takes its conclusion from the general given the specific, and the other does vice versa … or so my left-brain logically thinks.*

In ancient *Zen Buddhism*, intelligible sound was as *dependent* by the *lack* of sound (silence) in between syllables, as it is on the syllables themselves. Otherwise, one just has a long unintelligible monotone of sound, probably with differences, but otherwise unintelligible. *Have you ever received an eMail from someone who "forgets" to put in spaces, capitalization, and punctuation? Talk about unintelligible!* The same goes for music: the space between notes, and the timing, are as important as the notes themselves.

Thus the *Finite* world of duality defined by hot / cold, right / left, up / down, etc. – without both you have neither – is entered. And let's not forget *RIGHT / WRONG* as in **The McLaughlin Group**. Such is the world of duality as defined by the ego, or the logical word-oriented left-brain. Some insist the spaces *between* the music or words, etc. come from the *Infinite*. [9]

[9] Dyer, Dr. Wayne W. (2012-12-03). Getting In the Gap: Making Conscious Contact with God Through Meditation (p. 12). Hay House. Kindle Edition.

To start with, there is omnipresent infinity – there is no place that it is not. What qualifies something as *Infinite?* The basic characteristics are: it is invisible and non-physical. Next, no matter what you multiply or divide it by, you get the same thing. Let's take some examples. Do you know no matter how many times you multiply or divide it, you still get *possibilities?* Ditto for *silence* and limitless *energy*. But let's go back to the visible, physical stuff in our Universe.

Finally, let me give the easy question: Where does all this stuff come from? Presumably you are sitting down reading this, unless you like reading standing up. *Not that you have to be sitting down to read this, like somebody tells you to sit down before they tell you somebody died!* So maybe there's some kind of chair. Maybe it has arms and a back. Everything is optional.

Also assume there is some kind of light you are reading by; you may be in a room with walls. If so, there are probably one or more windows. If you look out the window, there may be grass and trees with or without leaves depending on the season, or you could be looking at a city street with asphalt, sidewalks, cars and people – maybe some trees with or without leaves.

Regardless of whether or not you are reading sitting down or standing up, you are surrounded by "stuff." So, once again, where does all this stuff come from? A generation or two ago there would have been a well-accepted answer, and it's still in widespread use today *although growing smaller, at least in this country or Western societies – [the big G-Man]*. Spoiler alert: if the "G" word freaks you out, skip over the next paragraph.

Yes, "[the big G-Man]" is "God" *(Allah, Buddha, or any other name humanity might choose to fight for a couple millennia over)*. Dr. Wayne Dyer says, in information related to him by a guru, every reference to God, whatever the word is, has the sound "ah" in it [10] ... but, for the sake of this writing, I AM summarily ruling this particular word OUT. Hence the God word itself is out, since any more people freaking out or wars are not needed. Besides, such an answer does not tell us much, and we're going other places. You will find references in this reading to God that look like this: "[the big G-Man]."

So where *does* all this stuff come from? If [the big G-Man] is ruled out, then where else does it come from? The truth is, stuff comes from the perceiver's, well, perception. And to complicate this further, a lot of perceptions are shared with everyone else in our Universe (i.e. reality). *Regardless of the person causing the accident because they swear the stop sign was not in their Universe.*

Deepak Chopra says in his book ***The Future of [the big G-Man]***

Perception defines reality. [11]

Chopra defines reality by perception in his book, so let's look a little deeper ... it's significant.

You are currently reading about reality, and four something per some time-frame perceptions are *available* to each of us in that time-frame. Others have different interpretations of how many perceptions are available to us consciously, and what the time-frame is, but this is adequate for our discussion.

Whether it is four-thousand per second, or four-million per hour, or what, it is four something per some time-frame, and it is a lot. So let's call it four-thousand per minute, even if it is four-thousand per second. *Let's face it, four-thousand perceptions per minute*

---

[10] Dyer, Dr. Wayne W. (2012-12-03). Getting In the Gap: Making Conscious Contact with God Through Meditation (p. 32). Hay House. Kindle Edition.

[11] Chopra, Deepak (2014-11-11). The Future of God: A Practical Approach to Spirituality for Our Times (Kindle Locations 1062-1063). Potter/ TenSpeed/Harmony. Kindle Edition.

divided by 60 seconds per minute gives us ... firing up the calculator app ... sixty-six and two-thirds perceptions per second. And that's a lot! Some will have less or more regarding what perceptions they think are available or perceived in reality.

Such perceptions would involve, say, the ambient air temperature, whether there is some breeze blowing across the hairs on your arm, available light, anyone else around, etc. These perceptions don't even involve what the individual cells *inside* your body are doing, or else it would be four-billion per second.

Perceptions of what is going on inside our body are mostly out-of-touch to us, including for the most adept, who regulate their own breathing, heartbeat, etc. And there are those who supposedly bypass the physical "laws" of our Universe and levitate, but "I'll believe *that* when I see it," as they say! Or is it "I'll see it when I believe it?"

With all this going on, how do four-thousand per minute *potential* perceptions get simplified to "I'm cold?" Forget where you are: the chair, the room and the window *(as you probably already have)* unless there is some specific reason to take notice of them. Your awareness would even accept lying to yourself about it. *Lying fades from your attention once it becomes pathological, but will probably rise to the level of your attention if your pants are on fire.*

Our brain is the most complex computer anyone could ever imagine, by a factor many times over. "Many times over" is not a multiplier here, but an exponent, and the result is really, really, big. So take the most complex computer you can imagine, and make it almost infinite. Because your brain can't be truly infinite, it is only *linked* to the *Infinite*. Even the most simple computer needs to be programmed to work, so guess what the brain needs?

Our brain has been "programmed" along the way by many people, which includes filtering out and ignoring all but the most pressing issues ... the rest get taken care of sub-consciously.

Important issues raised to our conscious attention might involve the proverbial fight-or-flight issues. They are often referred to as "fight, flight, or freeze!"

Speaking of freezing, our after-filter issues might be something less stressful than the original perceptions, and the result is something like "I'm freezing," prompting you to put on another layer of clothes. Filtering perceptions in or out of our awareness works really well, and pares down the available stimulations from four-thousand per minute to a few.

Filtering is, of course, ultimately related to our programming. What is filtered out in one's programming *(say, screaming kids)* raises a red-flag for others. Note the parent with the screeching kid being seemingly unconcerned with what is driving everyone else crazy. *Especially at the hair salon or on an airplane! A mother literally responded to "How do you stand it?" with "I just tune it out." Everyone else is not so lucky, but earplugs work good as filters in such a situation.*

Anything that attempts to explain mass consciousness programming (issues like gravity often seem to be built in or "just there") has yet to be encountered, but there must be somebody working on it. *Or they will be, now that they've read this! At the very least, they will be applying for a Government grant.* Cataloging things like gravity is a left-brain activity applied to the right- side.

Todays' technologies reveal at what brain wave frequency (and at what ages) are best for being programmed or re-programmed. Suffice it to say, most programming happens at an early age, and takes place via our parents or care-givers. Let's just hope they weren't too negative.

Regardless of how positive or negative they were, they were only human … but *right now*, at this very moment, we are learning how to change our life for the better. According to current knowledge of the brain, there are now techniques that make it easier to *re*-program our brain.

One important note about filtering. Filtering works not only in a hypnotist sense, where beliefs programmed (filtered) are pushed down into our sub-conscious. Filtering also works with all the stuff surrounding us on a moment-by-moment basis. There goes a co-worker with the nice, well, let's just say the particular detail of the co-worker rose to our attention for a too-brief moment. All the pens, papers, and stapler normally filtered out of our consciousness anyway became further so, but now the computer screen comes back into focus.

Infinity provides infinite possibilities, which then get merged with energy. This changes the energy in such a way as to make the ideas visible to us (or as the Law of Attraction states, attracts them to us), so they are accepted as "real." Along the way, our beliefs and ideas from mass consciousness get incorporated into our reality. The *Power of Consciousness* has taken us from the *Infinite* to the *Finite*.

There is a book called **Zen Driving**, which states the issue of programming / filtering nicely. It hypothesized: suppose you are driving along minding your own business, then someone driving a red-sports-car does something "uncouth," like cutting you off. *My special addition would be they flipped you the bird while doing it!* They "made you so mad," before long you might notice everyone else driving a red-sports-car was driving rudely, *even if they were not flipping everybody off.*

Filtering assures you would miss everyone else driving a red-sports-car courteously, doing things like waving people in ahead of them, etc. Such is the nature of the way mind filtering works, and it works really well.

Then there's a kicker. Sometime after your newly programmed filter is in effect, you will actually *attract* people driving red sports

cars discourteously *(or is it uncourteously – not nicely, regardless).*
BTW, you attracted the original driver too! **Zen Driving** was read
long before understanding anything about Quantum or spiritual
anything. Traditional thinking leads to: "Well, how can *that* be?"

No matter what anyone else does to you, no-one else can "make
you mad" or make you anything else, unless you surrender your
power to them. This would be the power you have to control your
own emotions, and the part of your brain controlling your link to
the *Infinite*. Then you attract things to reinforce the emotion.

If you surrender your power to someone else, they will "make you
mad" or make you anything else emotional, which surrenders
your creativity at the same time. By making you mad, they also
made you surrender your creativity! Whenever you hear someone
say "They made me so <something emotional>," don't listen to
them, or at least listen with a smile. It's like the old saying about
forgiveness: "*Not* forgiving is like taking poison and expecting the
other person to die." You are turning your power over to someone
or something else.

In the poison case, lack of forgiveness makes you technically
insane. Remember, one definition of insanity is doing the same
thing over and over, again and again, and expecting different
results. So just keep *not* forgiving them and eventually they will
die. And eventually they *will* die. So *not* forgiving is not so insane
after all, is it? *Plus they made you mad!*

Have you noticed lately that you will eventually die, too? Maybe
sooner than the non-forgiven one *(so you'll miss out on that part
of the satisfaction)*, especially if you are running around with
vengeance, hatred or any of the other non-forgiveness items going
on in your head. In any event, running around with negativity in
your head *will* make your life miserable. Your life is your creation,
guaranteed, no money back – and the preceding conclusion is not
insane at all.

So after all this discussion, where *does* the stuff come from you see when you open your eyes anyway? It comes from your perceptions, and your brain doing its duty via programming and filtering. Your brain has been programmed exclusively by others at an early age, then more and more it's under your own control. *Re*-programming is completely under your control, at whatever older age you might decide to do so.

Ultimately stuff comes from your perceptions, and sharing some perceptions with others, whose brains are doing the exact same thing, but for them – perceiving, filtering, and forming *their* reality.

The driving stuff is from, at least according to the book title, *Zen* philosophy. *Zen* has been around the Far East for a long, long, time. In the West, "Quantum Physics" and the "Law of Attraction" are around now.

It works much better when everyone agrees the stop sign is actually there.

Physics, Astronomy, and Sports

Today the planetary model of the atom is popular. We'll use Hydrogen (the first atom, with 1 *Electron*, 1 *Proton*, and 1 *Neutron*) for the model. Models and analogies make what would otherwise be unintelligible – understandable. In this model, the atom has a "Sun" (*Nucleus*) in the middle consisting of a *Proton* and *Neutron* the size of a softball, and the single "Planet" (Electron) is the size of a golf-ball orbiting the sun at the distance of 100 yards – a football field. *If you're one of the few still existing "flat earthers" you'll have to get your own model. But even flat earthers have football!*

The important part to remember in this model, regardless of whatever types of balls are involved, is there is a whole lot of empty space between the "Sun" and the "Planet." And the electron isn't made of anything anyway! It is simply a negative electrical charge, and the proton has a positive charge. Hence Hydrogen's place on the Periodic Table of Elements is 1.

Even with all the space in the middle, the atom's exterior "shell" is given to be "solid" in the model, presumably because the electron is going so fast. With the electron going all around the nucleus, it doesn't continue to orbit in the same plane as do actual planets, so there goes the planetary model – *ask any astronomer. Plus, 100 yards is a goodly distance in any classroom.*

But the model still has 100 yards between the Sun and the Planet (and that's only ½ the distance!) A football field is a large distance between a softball and golf-ball as any sports enthusiast will attest. That's a lot of space between the nucleus and electron(s) in an atom. *Especially when the electron is an electrical charge ... basically nothing at all!*

A couple Styrofoam balls for Hydrogen are connected to another larger Styrofoam ball by a couple straws, and *voila!* water (H_2O) is born. "O," Oxygen, is eight (8 electrons, Protons, and Neutrons) on the Periodic Table. *So a bigger Styrofoam ball for "O" is used.*

To maintain the analogy, you would have to stretch it a bit. For the heavier atoms, you would need basketballs and bowling balls (representing the "gas giants") to stay within the planetary model, but by then you could not make them into molecules using straws – you would probably need pipes. The larger balls' atomic weight would just be too much. Thus the plumber's crack is stealthily introduced.

The important thing to remember is: the atom, and molecules made out of atoms, are comprised of basically nothing. Space and electrical charges and one-or-more pesky little things called Neutrons complete the atom. In the ***Don Juan series*** by Carlos Castaneda, there are supposedly those who walk through walls, *but it's just another one of those in the long list of could-care-less items. I'll see it when I believe it.*

What do they say, "Seeing is believing?" What about "Believing is perceiving?" How about "I'll perceive it when I believe it?" Maybe the seeing-perceiving-believing statements work backwards and forwards.

The more advanced we become, the smaller and smaller, or conversely, the bigger-and-bigger (or farther) we will know about one theory says. "Today's facts are indistinguishable from the miracles of yesterday," they also say. Therefore, the Hubbell space telescope and electron microscopes are the scientists' toys of today; what the toys will be tomorrow, who knows? It was not long ago our Galaxy, the Milky Way, was all there was to the Universe, and the atom was the smallest thing going. Today … not so much, *especially if you're a Trekkie or a Quantum Physicist and Photons and Quarks are in your working vocabulary.*

There have been whole documentaries about how ideas (key is: "ideas") from **Star Trek** became reality like the wireless flip-phone communicator. In **Star Trek: The Next Generation** they just tap their chest to communicate, *so I'm assuming tapping your chest is a future cell-phone.* In both Star Trek series they had a transporter … but I'm still waiting on *that.* Which brings up yet another popular saying: "If you can see it, and believe it, you can achieve it."

The transporter was on **Star Trek** (the seeing part) … apparently we're just waiting on someone to believe it, because engineers can make anything (the achieving part). In fact, it wouldn't surprise me at all if there were engineers working on Transporters in their garage. The Personal Computer (PC) started out in somebody's garage. Before, they were just ideas in somebody's head. Not really in their head *per se*, but that's a whole 'nother story.

Not long ago, the wireless phone was just a gleam in somebody's mind *(there go those mixed-metaphors again!)* Today you can find the whole time-line for the invention of the phone (string, wire, wireless, et al) at Wikipedia on your wireless smart phone. *(Looking up the history of the phone on your smart-phone – ain't that a hoot?)* In terms of the phone itself, the initial ideas were way before cars, so the only use for the garage *then* was to invent stuff in. *Some people must currently have transporters in their garage, but not the car variety. Imagine the "Toyota Transporter." I've just given Toyota a futuristic-sounding model-name! Dibs on the copyright. Who wants to put money on what car-company uses the name first? I've got Toyota. Beam me up!*

Back to the atom and electrons, which are basically nothing, and molecules made of atoms. Then molecules build our visible Universe. So why do walls and tables appear so solid, and our tables hold our *half full or half empty* glass? At first glance, you must perceive the table as solid. *Have you ever known someone who always sees the glass as half full or half empty? Seeing is believing.*

Perceiving something one way, then the same way, then again, we will come to believe it is so. Or looking at the statement in reverse, our beliefs dictate appearances. The programmed belief comes first ... then the belief reinforces and provides supporting evidence for itself.

A belief is simply a thought, thought over and over and over again.[12] Sounds suspiciously like our programming makes the belief automatic, and thereby gets shoved down to our sub-conscious, where our filters operate with it. Maybe the thought becomes part of mass consciousness, and only rises to our attention as necessary. *Or our pants are on fire.*

First you have to think about driving a clutch and practice, but eventually it becomes, shall we say, "automatic." At that point it becomes as easy as driving an automatic, until you have to stop on an up-hill, and the person behind you stops so close they only give you a couple inches. *BTW (by-the-way for oldsters) the parking brake might be necessary for a stopping-on-a-hill situation, even for cars with automatic transmissions. Then you might have to think about what to do, like using the parking brake in conjunction with the clutch or transmission.*

Your pants were on fire from telling your parents you didn't go anywhere the weekend they were away. Just before the week your father had to replace the clutch in the family wagon. Fathers have to replace clutches so often anyway, don't they? Your pants-on-fire rises to the level of everybody's attention. Your father knew anyway – parents are smart like that!

Invisible possibilities merge with inexhaustible energy, pass through other cultural mass consciousness, and on down to be processed by our brain's programming, beliefs and filters. Energy,

[12] Hicks, Esther; Hicks, Jerry (2009-09-01). The Vortex: Where the Law of Attraction Assembles All Cooperative Relationships (p. 221). Hay House. Kindle Edition.

not being able to be created nor destroyed, changes its form and provides us with something visible, thereby bringing the idea back to us as a perception in our reality.

There is a saying in scripture:

> *"What is seen was not made out of things that are visible" [Hebrews 11:3]* [13] *or*
>
> *"The visible comes from the invisible."*

So starting with an idea, adding beliefs programmed into, and filtered by, our conscious and sub-conscious, turns some invisible energy into visible stuff. Atoms (basically nothing) turn into molecules, which go on to build our visible Universe. Now our reality becomes our perception of reality, and the idea and beliefs reinforce themselves.

Like the famous commentator said:

> *"And that's the rest of the story!"*

... but read on anyway for the quiz (kidding)

---

[13] Crossway Bibles (2011-02-09). The Holy Bible, English Standard Version (Kindle Location 47760). Good News Publishers/Crossway Books. Kindle Edition.

I spend ALL my kids inheritance

Upon learning Physics, the atom was the smallest unit in nature, even as teachers taught us sub-atomic particles known as *protons, neutrons,* and *electrons.* The sub-atomic parts of the atom were the smallest *particles.* Even though knowledge of even smaller "elementary particles" predates my education (Einstein was working on them), the atom was (and still is) the building block of the Universe, comprising our physical reality.

Quantum Physics is a branch of science developing over the last hundred years or so. It was around as they taught us the Styrofoam-ball atom and molecule planetary model. Photons are known as "elementary particles" that exhibit both the characteristics of particles (with mass) and waves (energy only), as per the research surrounding them. You may be familiar with the split wave – particle duality research. But Physics *(and Star Trek)* is used only for reference.

Between when Newton got bopped on the head by an apple and started Physics back in the day, and the current age of Quantum Physics, along came science. All the branches: chemistry, biology, etc. and more recently electronics or electrical physics. Science had a bunch of things in common: equations, units of measure, postulates, hypothesis, the scientific method and so on … and gave us predictability.

> *The day science begins to study non-physical phenomena, it will make more progress in one decade than in all the previous centuries of its existence.* [14]

---

[14] Proctor, Bob (2015-06-09). The ABCs of Success: The Essential Principles from America's Greatest Prosperity Teacher (Kindle Locations 1920-1921). Penguin Publishing Group. Kindle Edition.

There was *yet* another thing all the sciences had in common: they were completely removed from mind. I AM referring to spiritual mind, not the organ on the left side of the brain involved in intelligently solving equations.

Werner von Braun (a brilliant scientist taken from the NAZIs at the end of WWII and shipped to the US) is widely reputed to be the father of America's space program. He said the equations / laws-of-science were so precise as to be able to send a man to the moon and return him safely, which was ultimately done *if you do not believe in the conspiracy theory whereby the Moon Landing was all done in a film studio.*

As it goes, there are now sub-atomic "elementary particles" like quarks and photons. The Super-collider in Europe is larger than a Cathedral (not counting the ring itself), and it only catches mathematical traces of what physicists suppose is there. Such is the nature of Quantum Physics.

When you go ripping around a ring nearing the speed-of-light before you crash head-on, it's not the same as a car crashing into a bench full of people waiting for the bus. A car has yet to be invented that gets near the speed of light, and by then you would have learned driving a clutch and using the parking brake on a hill and how not to crash into benches full of people.

The planetary model of the atom has Styrofoam balls representing atoms, and straws connecting them into molecules. The electrons were orbiting the atom so fast, for all intents and purposes the atom was solid – like a Styrofoam ball – except you could punch a straw into it. *There needed to be something connecting Styrofoam atoms into a molecule, so that's how straws got invented.*

The Quantum Physics model of the atom is different from the planetary model. The electron, instead of being at a distinct place in an "orbit" having what engineers would call a "vector," it (or they) now reside in what Quantum Physicists call a "probability cloud." The electron(s) position is related to wherever the observer *expects it to be.* Now the electron, an integral part of the atom itself (remember, the atom is the building block of nature), is now intimately linked to the observer, and thereby so is nature and reality (the physical Universe) itself.

An interesting dilemma develops. Assuming Quantum Physics is a science, it should share traits with other sciences like predictability, but it's only been around for the last century or so. It also incorporates the *Infinite*, which has no predictability whatsoever. Try predicting inspiration or coincidence. Not happening. *BTW, if you can accurately predict sports outcomes, let me know!*

Before Quantum Physics, science gave us predictions, but was completely removed from mind. This has been true since Sir Isaac Newton got bopped on the head by an apple. In the age of Quantum Physics, personal beliefs are intimately linked to the observable. Yesterday, mind was out. Today, mind is in. For all the sciences prior to Quantum Physics, the reasoning left-brain with its equations was always in. In Quantum Physics, reasoning, predicting, *et al* is not as much involved ... the right-brain is right there. *OK, I won't highlight the puns.*

It seems older religions were always *all* mind and therefore un-measurable. Religion has now met science which never had any "mind" (reason only) but had all those equations, predictions, and units of measure. So there must be *something* in religion that would affirm "there is something similar to Quantum Physics that has *always* been in religion." *Right?*

Let's start by taking some of the major western organized religions in linear time order. First there's *Judaism*, the first major western religion, evolving from polytheism some time ago. Why would any religion have to be monotheistic to fit the mold? In monotheism, there is only *one law* applying to everything. Therefore, there is not a separate law of gravity for the Sun, one for the Earth, and one for the Moon; likewise there cannot be separate Deities with their own laws for the Sun, Earth, and Moon. This automatically eliminates polytheism, where each Deity has its own set of laws.

Judaism has its scriptures, known as the Tora (or in the Judeo-Christian world it is the Old Testament of the **Bible**). They communicated their philosophy via stories, and there were plenty of them. Moses was talking to a burning bush that was not consumed by fire about some commandments; Noah built an Ark with two of everything on board *(nobody knows why he didn't leave ticks and mosquitos out)*; the Red Sea was parted; and Lott's wife turned into a pillar-of-salt by looking backwards *(mirrors were yet to be invented)*.

The 10 Commandments were as much about morals as anything else. *You know the ones that go something like: Don't go lusting after your neighbor's wife (and his other stuff) and don't go knocking him off if nothing else works. That's just to name a couple Commandments. There were originally more than 10, but some editor said no-one would ever read more than 10, even if they were carved in stone. So there became 10. Plus it's easy to remember ... ten, that is, not the Commandments.*

Then Jesus came along, and *Christianity* evolved later. Their scriptures are known as the *New Testament*. They were still into telling stories via their philosophy, and there were stories about Jesus walking on water, calming the seas, curing the ill, raising the dead, and multiplying the loaves and fishes, just to name a few. Today, after all this science, you have to go to a restaurant or other food source to multiply loaves and fishes, and the bill is correspondingly multiplied! *The left-brain does not seem to apply right-brain / religious stories to modern living.*

They had a couple good sayings paraphrased: *"It is done unto you as you believe;"* and one often referred to as "The Golden Rule" states: *"Do unto others as you would have them do unto you."* Note they use "as" making the sayings present tense and active. *Of course, they used "ye" instead of "you" to make sure you knew you were reading scripture. "Ye" is easier to write than "you," but if that was done everywhere, it would make everything seem scriptural. So somebody invented fonts and italicizing instead. The "unto" part is left in here for scriptural purposes.*

Muslims must have their stories too. Mohammed entered a cave, and was commanded to write the **Koran**. If he had gone into a trance, and a non-physical entity spoke through him with someone else transcribing, it would be much the same as todays channeled material.

Stories were the way religions made their point pre-equation and measurements. For instance, male and female properties in everything was one of the objects of the Noah's Ark lesson. Then the Dark and Middle Ages came along, Newton got bopped on the head by an apple, and he brought us science. Mind was out; reason was in, along with equations, measurements, and predictions *et al. Along the way, someone invented linear time, so there could be watches and stress. I think therapists invented time, watches and stress – plus the 50-minute hour!*

Science has weights and measures *(which the British "royally" screwed up – who puts 12 "inches" in a "foot?"),* equations and predictability. Religion has mental stuff like faith and prayer, but how do you measure *them? (Maybe British lawyers could put 12 prayers in a quid-pro-quo.)* Then along comes Quantum Physics to represent reality, as religion was always purported to have done in different ways than equations. Shouldn't there be a trace of Quantum Physics in what the stories of religion always had, back in the day before science?

See if you can pick out the science (equations, hypothesis, scientific method and predictability, etc.) in: Moses talking to a burning bush (and vice versa), Noah putting two-of-everything in an Ark (with a limited time to build and stock it), or someone parting an ocean. To say nothing of morals as stated in the 10 Commandments which are carved in stone, no less. *Why hasn't anyone been successful finding them, except in* **Raiders of the Lost Ark** *where they melted NAZIs faces off?* The Commandments, based on words, are totally "reasonable," *leaving it to government lawyers aka politicians aka Priests to find loopholes. Especially if you pay them enough.* But science they're not.

Similarly, see if you can find the science in: walking on water, calming the seas, curing the ill (only by touching the hem of His garment, and not by some pill Big Pharma markets on TV by its color) and – my personal favorite – raising the dead.

What equations would you use for raising the dead? How would you measure the results? Were they really dead? People have been known to get better from being dead, hence the term "dead ringer." And what side-effects could be listed on a commercial for a "purple pill" that raises the dead? Certainly one of the side-effects could not be "Causes occasional death!" Talk about a zombie craze! Could you get mind if you ate enough brain? Maybe what is needed are more purple pills ... or better yet, some blue ones!

Would you believe people are still looking for "proof" (in a scientific way) of Noah's Ark? They occasionally find something they are sure is it, on the side of some mountain somewhere in Turkey. And they're still looking for proof of traces of "The Great Flood," now that they can look from space. *Gotta love them scientists.*

They actually have found scientific evidence of a meteorite leaving a dent on the floor of the Indian Ocean, evidenced by a decrease in the sea-level topside (however they measure *that!*) Resulting tsunamis left impressions when viewed from space, looking like the impression waves will leave on sand when viewed close-up. Scientists are still trying to "figure out" (i.e. prove) if a meteorite hit gave us the "Great Flood" or not, in order to scientifically prove or disprove religious stories.

There may be some validity to proving some religious stories, which ironically might come right-back-around to "prove" the theory that consciousness creates reality. How would that be? *Scientists may be even more interested in the meteorite crashing in the Ocean off the Yucatan Peninsula and wiping out the dinosaurs 67 million years ago, if only dinosaurs could be proved to have had religion, and there were an "Old-Old Dinosaur Testament" with stories! But don't worry, Dinosaurs come back with a vengeance in* **Jurassic Park** *(3D).*

Perhaps the underlying metaphysical (beyond physics) lessons represented by the stories should be examined, and then applied in a Quantum Physics style. Let's take an "oldie but goodie." It is a story most will be familiar with, if not from a religious standpoint, then from folklore. It is the story of "The prodigal son." [15]

For those not familiar with the story of "The prodigal son," here's a summarization: a wealthy father has two sons, who know they will inherit the father's wealth when he passes. The one son, we'll call him the *Impatient One*, desires his inheritance NOW. The father agrees and gives the inheritance to him, and the son proceeds to go out and spend it all. He slinks back home in shame, and the father accepts him back. Such is the gist of the story the vast majority knows.

From a basic religious standpoint, one learns the lesson of forgiveness ... the father forgives the son and accepts him back. Many have been taught an important lesson on forgiveness, and it *is* important. End of story. *Like the late-night-infomercial says, "But wait!"*

---

[15] Thomas Troward. Bible Mystery and Bible Meaning (Chapter XI. Forgiveness - Kindle Location 2066-2163). Kindle Edition.

R Preston Todd

The Impatient son *never* realizes the infinite nature of abundance, and so he spends all his money and never realizes our inheritance cannot be exhausted. So he spends it all, must return home in shame, and is forgiven. So goes the lesson, part A. Then New Thought comes along and advances the story a couple steps from what has been all but forgotten, and the Law of Attraction chimes in.

In part B of the story, another part the vast majority miss, the second son (we'll call him the *Patient One*) is totally ignored and stays home. The second son *never claims* his inheritance! He stays home, and might be totally aggravated as the first son comes back and is graciously received ... wouldn't most siblings be similarly inclined? But the infinite nature of abundance and the second son's feelings are not important to the story of forgiveness most know.

So now our story has two parts, and each part itself has two parts. By the way *(BTW for young-uns)*, can anybody yet name for me the scientific principle, complete with equations and predictability demonstrated in the story? So now let's explain the story a bit further, make it fit the Law of Attraction, and make it suitable as a lesson for the vast minority.

The first son, the *Impatient One*, NOW goes out, realizes the *Infinite* Law-of-Natural-Abundance-and-Prosperity, and never looks back. The Law of Attraction completes his mental picture so he will *never* return home in shame yet again; he not only *realizes* his abundance, but *expects* it and could-care-less about the second brother – *some things never change*. He puts his attention on thoroughly believing and *expecting* abundance while *allowing* his brother to do whatever he will with the second brother's inheritance.

The second son, the previously ignored *Patient One* who stayed home, says "Whoa! Wait a Minute!" This time he takes his

36

inheritance, realizes the endless infinity-of-abundance and his own *expectation* thereof, and splits without looking back. *Without even a "Thank You," the father notes. Such is the nature of being the parent of ungrateful children. "Oy vey!" the Father exclaims from his Jewish heritage.*

So now a complete story is philosophically meaningful; it went from *forgiveness* to *abundance* to *desire* to *claiming* it to *expecting* it to *allowing* others to do whatever they want. The complete circuit from a scripture story (which now includes Quantum Physics providing natural abundance, and the Law of Attraction doing the rest) with nary a scientific equation needed or wanted has been made. Philosophically, such is to be expected when religion makes a point through their stories.

If you didn't get the Quantum Physics part of the story, it is: both sons create their reality. They both influenced the probability cloud of electrons by their *attention* and *expectations*, which then become inherent in the building-block-of-nature atom … and their Universe. The atoms then go on to form molecules, and on up to reality itself. Quantum Physics would predict both sons created their reality, which then exhibits the evolution of consciousness.

In the more recent past, consciousness has evolved into yet another religion generically called "New Thought." One of the beliefs from New Thought: whatever is later made manifest in your reality, is first created in your mind. Some of the more popular "sects" are Christian Science (many know of the **Christian Science Monitor**), Religious Science, and Unity, and in-the-middle between old and new religions are Quakers. Christians have always had *Catholics* and *Protestants* (*Baptists, Lutherans,* etc.) since they've been "reformed." *Reformed religions make jokes about, and wars with, other religions.*

New Thought has some of the trappings of the older organized religions, like someone-in-charge (Christians call them Priests or Ministers, New Thought calls them Pastors) and particular times and methods for services (Sunday morning) and prayer (Religious Science calls them "treatments"). New Thought sects use other labels for the same things. Then along comes Quantum Physics and the Law of Attraction.

Thus is the nature of reality versus what your kids expect from you. Tell them to *expect* it from their own physical Universe instead! So if your kids complain about you spending all their inheritance, tell them you have a story for them.

> *The bumper sticker says: "I spent all my kids'*
> *inheritance."*

One July Day

It was one week after my eighth birthday, and I was **Home Alone** with my Father who had stayed home ill from work. He had come home sick the day before, and was in bed awaiting the Doctor (they still made house calls then). My Mother was at work down the street, and my instructions were to call her when the Doctor arrived – they still used rotary-dial-phone numbers like MAyflower 1-1776.

My Father had type-1 diabetes from birth, the kind they have not yet "cured," and he was more-or-less happy with the insulin needle thing he had to do. But the Doctor said "Oh, you have to take this oral medication instead" and so my Father did. *Short story long,* "Here yesterday, gone today" courtesy of Big Pharma.

There was recently a TV ad for an insulin / diabetes pill, so Big Pharma is still at it. *Market the pill by its color only, while there are still some unique colors left.* On today's 60 second ads, if it says what it does in 20 seconds, they use the other 40 seconds to list all the side-effects. *But don't worry, they have a pill for the side-effects too! One says "Don't take this if you're allergic to it!" A sleep-aid side-effect says "in rare cases, can cause death." Do you really need to hear that from a sleep-aid? Not to worry – now they have a pill that cures death, too.*

If our society was litigious back then, today there'd be one more rich lawyer and I'd probably be in as good a shape as Joey Coyle who "found" bags of money after they flew out of the back of an Armored Truck somewhere around Philadelphia (see the movie **Money for Nothing** – *spoiler alert: he's dead, but now there's this pill*). My suggestion is: don't engage with Western Medicine or Big Pharma to any extent not necessary. I used to "blame" them when I was a victim, but now realize it is all part of the big picture. *Do* *you realize birth is the single leading cause of death? Marriage causes divorce?*

People have asked me if I feel in any way responsible for what happened. No; I had *just turned* eight … but still knew something wasn't right. To this day, some memories surrounding this event are vivid, but now the whole thing has become a learning experience. *What else am I going to do – complain about it? That would be about as effective as complaining when it's a rainy day … or too hot out … or too cold. Some people complain about everything, but now they're dead. Maybe they're allergic to a pill that cures death.*

The net result is: more and more I AM convinced "spirituality" is the important element forming one's own reality, *not* getting a good education and working hard aka "the Christian Work Ethic" like they taught us. *Didn't I say previously that everything was backward and upside-down? Eyeglasses with mirrors can fix that.*

The best explanation *Presbyterian* religion could come up with regarding my father's death was "Jesus needed him in Heaven." As an eight-year-old, I didn't need my Father whatsoever, if only Jesus needed him … *if I would have "understood" that then, I would still be Christian! I could also be gay! But there is something about being gay AND Christian that is mutually exclusive … OR gay and Muslim. Gotta love them religions!*

Way back they were preaching "Love, Peace, and Forgiveness," with only one caveat. If you did not believe in exactly the same manner they did, and use the exact same words in the same way, they were going to come over there and kill you. Religious wars didn't make sense to me then; religious fundamentalism still doesn't make sense to me now. So I didn't have any religion before "My great awakening." *Maybe I just took a purple pill, had a long dirt-nap, and was just getting better after being dead for a while.*

After my spiritual awakening, if what religious leaders were saying was true, then everyone else in our culture who were still following

"Organized Religion", needed awakening too, but later came to believe whatever level of spirituality you have is OK ... even none at all. You can even be *atheist* or *agnostic* if you want. *Did you hear the one about the dyslexic atheist agnostic who wondered if there was any proof there was a dog? Woof!*

You can call it spirituality or whatever term you like. *At the end of the disclaimers in the commercial for the chartreuse spirituality pill, it says "Death is guaranteed, whether you take the pill or not!" and this covers everyone. Life's a beach and then you die!*

Since "My Great Awakening," I learned *Transcendental Meditation (TM)*, and studied channeled teachings or philosophies including *The Seth Material, Pathwork,* and most lately Abraham and the *Law of Attraction.* Although not channeled, *Religious Science* teachings and readings have been there, as well as reading, listening, and watching Dr. Wayne Dyer materials.

Recently a technique called *Emotional Freedom Technique (EFT)*, popularly called "Tapping" has been learned, using ancient Chinese energy meridians utilized by acupuncture and acupressure to use the body's own energy to address various problems. EFT is supposedly scientifically validated.

Countless works over the years have been read and studied, including those by: Deepak Chopra, MD, Eckhart Tolle, the *Don Juan series* by Carlos Castaneda, and many other *Religious Science* and *Law of Attraction* series and materials, among others – some of them many times over.

Every media has been engaged including: books (formerly of the "dead tree" variety, moving on to Kindle eBooks and as replacements); TV (video, movies, specials, documentaries, telethons); computer (PDFs and other downloads, podcasts and other "training" sessions); and other audio and video (MP3s, MP4s, and the like). The one notably absent and currently popular one goes by the name of "social media" – *Facebook, Twitter, etc.*

R Preston Todd

These are methods of connecting with other people, and not learning *per se* to my knowledge. Maybe these would be useful via links to what others are learning, but these currently do not interest me as there's only 24 hours in a day! *Could I have a programmed belief in time limitation? Not to worry, death cures that!*

The best teacher is by *demonstrating*, and even more is learned while I write. It is in this spirit a composite of all the learning materials absorbed over-the-years is presented, going beyond learning to demonstrate my view of the evolution of consciousness.

As the (final) release step in a Science of Mind treatment goes:

> *And so it is!*

The multi-dimensional Roadmap

Long ago I developed an analogy using the 2-dimensional paper roadmap. After the roadmap analogy is fully developed and multi-dimensional, it then represents the Akashic records. Many don't know of the Akashic records, although they are referenced by "psychics" of many kinds, on purpose or not.

A folded up roadmap can be procured at most gas stations, covering an area of your choosing: either nation-wide, a particular state, or more local. You will also find more detailed maps on the back. If you look in the right places, you will find a spiral-bound notebook with much of the same information represented therein, maybe on a state-by-state basis for the whole country.

In case you don't know, C7 goes to C7 on some other map if you can ever find it. You can even get highlighted and specially prepared maps of the route you will take going from point A to point B from triple-A (AAA – Automobile Association of America). It's easier to find C7 because of the highlighting. AAA is not to be confused with AA nor A. AA is, of course, Alcoholics Anonymous. Stevie Wonder sang the motto: "Don't-a drive-a drunk." I was kind-a' hopin' he wasn't a-drivin' sober either. It's the number of As that matter.

The same mapping and direction information is now presented on-screen by a lot of on-line map services like *Google, Yahoo!* and *MapQuest*, with additional instructions. You can zoom in and out, overlay your map with satellite imagery, but it remains 2-D on your computer. You can print the directions out on paper *(where they remain 2-D, because paper is 2-D)*, and fold it up as small as you want for your convenience. You can store and then choose different starting locations on your computer, since the mapping software theoretically does not know where you are. *I say theoretically, because "they" really know where you are, but I'm not actually paranoid. You know what "they" say: "It's not paranoia if it's actually happening!"*

You can enter your destination into your car GPS, since the car already knows where it is *(so do "they," whoever "they" is)*, and the instructions on getting from <wherever-the-car-is> to the destination are given in a pleasing voice of your choosing. Some more advanced systems offer real-time directions around traffic-jams or detours. All this fits nicely into the analogy, except maybe the pleasing voice.

Here's how the analogy goes: You are sitting at your kitchen table with a map spread out before you, or maybe you are in your GPS enabled car, or maybe you are somewhere at a computer. Wherever you are, here you are, at your starting location (you need to start somewhere). This fits nicely with the Law of Attraction as explained by Abraham.

If you don't know where you are going in any of the preceding situations, you will get nowhere *fast* via our Roadmap, but at least it's *somewhere* … right? You will get the same place (nowhere) by the car GPS or a regular roadmap. But let's suppose you start driving anyway … you can't just go nowhere. If you start in Chicago and go *one* way, you will drive into Lake Michigan. Any other way you will either: run out of gas somewhere, or maybe go round-and-round and end up someplace you can walk or hitch-hike home. In the analogy, this is creating your life by default as known by terms the Law of Attraction often uses.

But let's continue to suppose you are starting in Chicago. You have always wanted to see Miami and visit the Everglades, so you start south, more-or-less. You are on a highway headed southeast, with the car on cruise-control, and you even take your hands off the wheel, the car is so in alignment. Before long, you have forgotten your original intention to see Miami, *and are asleep.* Once again, you are creating your trip (life) by default. To quote some lyrics:

> *"Drivin' with your eyes closed, there's gonna' be a crash, everybody knows!"*
>
> **Building the Perfect Beast; Don Henley**

Let's take a little closer look at the Roadmap-of-Life itself.

Anyone who has ever looked at a roadmap is probably familiar with some numbered routes running together. There is a state or federal symbol with two numbers inside it, or a federal symbol with a number and different federal symbol and number (i.e. Interstate vs. US route) close by on the same road-line, or a state symbol with a different number on the same section as a federal route, with none turning off.

On a roadmap, this indicates two or more separate routes running together for a while, before they split apart. If you look *far enough ahead*, and both are headed in the same direction, they may run together again. *Some people keep going back for do-overs.*

In life, two or more lives running together for a while indicates a shared goal: like, say, dating, getting married, and raising a family. The route number would eventually be the same. After the kids are gone, the parents get divorced and the routes split in real life. In any event, when the kids are big enough to get their own numbers, they go off in their own direction (and start to run together with other routes) … *before they boomerang home to a parent's basement!*

A couple numbered routes running together might also indicate a business partnership. It might even take on the same number, for a while at least. When the business dissolves, partners go in their own separate directions with their own numbers, *especially if one stole all the money!* Many individuals coming together in a corporation or an enterprise might warrant its own Interstate number.

Take, for instance, I-95 now going from ME to FL. This could be Microsoft. Apple computer could have, for the longest time, been route 1 going the same way to the same places, only slower and more scenic. Nowadays, AAPL (Apple's stock symbol) has branched out in many different directions and established their own Interstates with their own numbers.

If a map were to have a third dimension, up and down *(or "Z" coordinates for those mathematically inclined)* and not just flat, you will readily see where this analogy would then accommodate many more circumstances. Now expand it into infinite dimensions, and you will see it fits any and all circumstances, as in the Akashic records. In infinity, everybody gets their own map which may intersect anyone else's. *Infinity is infinite.*

Like any map, you need to start somewhere and have a definite destination (goal) in mind for it to be of any use whatsoever, and there is nothing preventing you from changing your mind at any time! You can be headed south from Chicago, and decide to go east and see Washington, DC. It's still the same drill: start from somewhere and have a destination. To use a map you need to be specific.

Now that you have seen Washington, DC (maybe in the reality of life you have dated someone for a while), you can set your sights once again for the state of FL (the state of holy matrimony, *or maybe you're old and can eat dinner at 3:15 in the afternoon)*. Whether you both wanted to take the faster (MS) I-95, or the more scenic (AAPL) US-1, or go separate routes, the important part is your shared destination goal of FL. This is living your life on purpose.

But suppose you are NOT living your life on purpose. You may start from Chicago and head south with no specific destination. You go south for a while, then see a sign for something that looks interesting to the west. After you see something to the west, you may still remember you were headed south, and so start south again. Until you see something that looks interesting to the east, so you head off east. It wasn't all that interesting, so you keep going in the same direction – east – more or less. By now, you have forgotten you were originally headed south. You end up in Atlantic City or New York with no place east left to drive, and wonder how you got there! You have created your trip (life) by default.

Maybe a map will help you get back to Chicago from NYC – if you remember to use it. You always have a starting point – it is where you are. The question is, can you set an ending point (goal) and stick with the program? If so, you are guaranteed to get there ... but you can still make adjustments. As long as the detours and roadwork aren't too many and too random, you will be guaranteed to get where you are going. Persistence has it. *Sorry, real life has no money-back guarantee.*

But, as in life, too many adjustments will get you nowhere – this could indicate a lack of a goal. Or maybe a lack of persistence. Maybe both. *You search in vain for a money-back guarantee.*

Let's leave the Roadmap and go on a journey more like life itself complete with: road signs, streetlights, and coincidences. Life is more real than any map, and real things *are* on the trip you are taking. You're travelling down the road, and there's a sign: so far to wherever. If you've noticed the sign, in some instances you may also wonder "who could possibly care?" Somebody did. They probably even went there frequently. *If there's some fine-print on the sign, it was probably some lawyer-politician that went there.*

You may have noticed how disconcerting it is to travel a road without streetlights, especially if they are usually there, but this time the street is lit up. You feel better when the way is well lit, equivalent to having a goal and planning. On the Roadmap-of-Life, you are at least headed somewhere specific.

And coincidences – we've all had them, noticed or not. Knowing who the calling party is on the other end of a ringing phone before you answer it (without looking at Caller ID) is a popular one. Sometimes the answer to a problem arrives in a dream, which may be chalked up to coincidence. How else could you have possibly gotten an answer while you were fast asleep? Maybe the *Infinite* was co-operating with the left-side of your brain while you were asleep – *or else you could use the standard "I must've dreamed it!"*

First suppose you are a guy living your life by default, taking a job and dealing as best as possible to whatever comes your way, *plus deal with your co-workers!* He doesn't have a map, and probably wouldn't look at it if he did. His car doesn't have GPS, and he just hopes he can make it to wherever he is going every time he starts the car – if it starts anyway. "Did I remember to check the oil?" billowing clouds of blue-black smoke remind him.

Usually he makes it via a familiar route to one of his many jobs, driving with one headlight out after dark, barely noticing, until a Cop stops him. Most of the streetlights are out, but he also doesn't notice. He saw a street sign once and wondered "who the f-bomb cares how far it is to there, anyway?" So he stopped looking at street signs. He doesn't care anything about coincidences. Short lived happiness comes from paying his MasterCard with his Visa.

Now a second guy, let's call him the first guy's older brother, lives his life in the completely opposite manner, as brothers are apt to do. He has his mental map, filled with specific, measurable destination goals and waypoints, and is not afraid to adjust them if need be via spiritual guidance – serendipity, intuition and / or coincidences, etc. He has a fairly new car with GPS, and all the lights work well. His path is well lit, both by his headlights and working streetlights. He is well on his way to a planned destination.

The second brother's way is well lit, even if he adjusts his course *en route*, or just makes an unanticipated turn. There are also well lit overhead road signs, like on a highway, for whenever he is not using GPS, or as confirmation. The best part is: he can follow his hunch onto another route, even if it was not programmed into his car GPS. *His car GPS has a new feature called "hunches."* He is open-minded, flexible, but doesn't change his destination often.

He remembers one time he "had a hunch" to take an exit from the highway he was on, even though he was right-on-time for his meeting. It was after taking the exit he met his wife, who had a flat tire on the shoulder of the exit, so he stopped to help *(all right, she was good-looking and wearing a short summer dress!)* One might say "his hunch payed off!" He found out later the meeting had been postponed. *Coincidence or not – you be the judge.*

The younger brother was supposed to give a toast at the older ones wedding reception (he was not trusted with other best-man duties), but his car wouldn't start. *The brothers hate each other's guts anyway … such is family!*

If you live in NY, but have never been outside NY state *(there's lot's to see there, just ask the tourist bureau!)* … do you believe CA doesn't exist? Of course not! There's even a page in your spiral-bound map-book for CA that proves it. Let's take it one step further: there are no maps for Europe (or any other place outside the US) in your map-book, so do you believe other *countries* don't exist? *There was a flat-earth time when maps of known areas ended with you falling off the edge into dragons and danger, but not today.*

Do you believe anything not-in-sight or on the map you are using does not exist?

J.P. Morgan once said:

> *"Go as far as you can see … from there you can see farther."*

There are lots of people telling you to go a certain way, with other suggestions like: it's faster, or more scenic, *or you can make more money doing what they have never done, etc. Do you send off to triple-A for a highlighted map for every decision you must make? Do you listen to someone who has never done <whatever> telling you to do it? Seriously?*

A lot of people want a highlighted map for every decision they make, and they first turn away from the Roadmap-of-Life by listening to somebody else. There is wisdom to the effect: "a tourist sees everything everybody else wants them to see, and a traveler observes and learns."

The actual quote by Gilbert K. Chesterton is:

> *"The traveler sees what he sees, the tourist sees what he has come to see."*

Are you a tourist or a traveler in your own life? Think about it … it's *really safe* doing what somebody else says to do, and it's *even safer* to do what everyone else is doing.

> *"If it looks too good to be true, it usually is."*
>
> *Oops, wrong quote [background shuffling sounds] … there it is:*
>
> *"Every decision opens up a whole new Universe."*

What is meant by this in the Roadmap analogy: for every fork in the road, you go either right or left, and thereby choose another route number in your life; there are road signs (how far it is to some destination), and whether the road is well lit, etc. Remember, you are already *off* the Interstate and not just watching exits go by *(or asleep)*. You are now at a new waypoint on the Roadmap-of-Life. Whether it is a new starting point depends on your decision.

Creating a new Universe does not apply to minuscule decisions like whether to have a bologna or PBJ sandwich for lunch, *unless you got food poisoning and have to go to the hospital where you meet the nurse you married.* Every seemingly minor decision can become major, but most don't. *Stay alert to the bologna with some green on it. There are times when you really don't want to "GO green!"*

What definitely creates a new Roadmap page applies to decisions like: going on to college or taking a job; whether to take a particular job (and move) or keep looking; should I marry a particular person *(with all that implies)* or stay single and keep looking, etc. *A good decision would be to stay single – ask most married people! The grass is always greener on the other side of the fence – ask any horse.* But ultimately you must keep on moving, and the Roadmap accommodates all changes, should you care to have any goals at all. You don't need a roadmap just to be safe and blend into the crowd, doing what everyone else is doing.

Now let's take the analogy farther into the *Infinite,* farther into the Akashic records where there is no scientific proof available, nor will there ever be.

"In the infinite, anything is possible"

so let's look at a familiar example: the Wright Brothers take a short flight and "invent" the airplane.

Farther along our mapped-out journey into reality are jumbo jets, a moon landing, the Space Shuttle, 9/11, and the TSA to name a few waypoint pages. But suppose the Wright Brothers never took the initial flight at Kitty Hawk? *Orville decided to invent microwave popcorn instead, and changed his last name to Redenbacher.* Or maybe Wilbur didn't feel good that day, and somebody else "flew" first. Maybe they decided against doing something so bizarre and stayed in Ohio running their bicycle shop – all are possibilities in infinity.

Say somebody else invented an airplane with a tail looking more like (from today's familiar airplanes) a bird's tail, with elevators, ailerons, and rudder all in one moveable assembly. For those not familiar with airplane moveable control surfaces, don't worry about it. Everybody knows what a bird looks like. But I'm running right over to the patent office to patent the idea!

Somehow nature, evolving over millennia, had it more right than the Wright brothers *(pun wrightly intended)* even if flapping your arms covered in feathers didn't make it. At least natural evolution might have gotten it more right with regard to the "tail" assembly. *The wing-flapping thing, even if powered, never panned out, at least in this reality. But the tail assembly could have gone in an entirely different direction.*

On our Roadmap, there are roads running back together, with airplanes looking more like birds (at least regarding their tails) crashing into the World Trade Centers. Then again our reality could have no airplanes at all. "Come on" you would say, "Who would believe *that?*" Does the fact your reality map-book does not include Europe deny the existence of Paris?

Most of us think *our* reality is the only one … but is it? The next time you start your cerebral car, do you have a roadmap (or at least a GPS), and know where you are going?

The invisible to the visible

Let's start by assuming there is no creativity involved in either the *Infinite* or the *Finite*. Some say there is creativity involved in both, but that is their ego involved in classifying everything. Maybe a more correct term would be no *real* creativity, as in creating something brand new by "thinking outside the box."

There has been an effort, for longer than time itself has been around, to understand how things get from the invisible (a possibility, or an idea) to the visible (the results thereof) in our reality. This process of going from the invisible to the visible is life itself. The term *Power of Creation* keeps it from getting entangled with words about everything else. *BTW, if you have ever been Christian, "How's that Father, Son, and especially the 'Holy Ghost' thing been workin' out for ya?" to paraphrase Dr. Phil. Not to be blasphemous, but can anyone tell me what a "Holy Ghost" is anyway?* That's another reason for using different terms.

Something called "free will" (sometimes referred to as "free won't") opts us in or out of anything, especially guidance from the *Infinite*, aka intuition, serendipity, etc. The *Infinite* has our back, but our ego will often opt us out. Would always opting in contradict the notion of free will? Always opting in would imply predestination. Such is one of life's paradoxes, but it's easier to go with guidance from the *Infinite* than figure it all out solo.

Some attach the label of spirituality to the process of going from the *Infinite* to the *Finite*, others have other labels, sometimes of religious origin. It doesn't matter what label you attach, the effort is the same. And you are free to fight for a couple millennia over a word if you want. But understanding something only applies to the reasoning side of the brain.

53

Switching back to the *Infinite,* also to a subject many are not familiar with, "channeled" wisdom is knowledge coming from a non-physical entity (or entities), not otherwise having the ability to communicate with us. The entity speaks through someone known as a "channel" who enters a trance-like state, and is thereby able to speak directly as a non-physical entity. In some cases, questions are able to be directed to the entity through the channel, and the non-physical entity returns answers.

We are well advised not to take much of what might become available from different sources seriously, since every group has its frauds. The better known sources, at least the most popular ones, are those demonstrating their value. Inherently, knowledge provided through certain channeled sessions become valuable beyond knowing it from only our physical standpoint.

There is a very thin line between "channeled material," and what might otherwise be considered "*original* material," even if such writing might be taken to be "automatic writing," or some other term associated with religion or spirituality. One makes a shift along with changing terminology from "I wrote this" to "Creative Intelligence *is using me* to write this" to "I AM writing this <u>as</u> Creative Intelligence." You are now reading a work more toward the latter, because I don't know where it is coming from, nor how it proceeds from the invisible to the visible (*except apparently Creative Intelligence needs a spell-checker*). If you want a concrete example, try writing something and label where it came from.

The very first book ever purchased after my "Great Awakening" in the area of "higher consciousness," was the third book in a series known as the **Seth Material** called **The Nature of Personal Reality**. The series is very popular in the higher consciousness arena. The wisdom-filled series is channeled material, given by a consciousness-only entity known as Seth, through the in-trance channel of Jane Roberts, and written down verbatim by her husband, Robert Butts.

The series was a direct precursor to the currently popular series known as the ***Abraham series***, also channeled material by a number of entities known as Abraham. They are channeled through Esther Hicks, formerly with the direction of her husband Jerry. The sessions were recorded, some were transcribed, and later distributed in many forms. The series promotes what is now popularly known as the Law of Attraction. Both Seth and Abraham channeled wisdom, and the channels themselves came close to actually meeting.

In the ***Seth Material***, Seth asked Robert (through Jane) if he remembered being one of two male siblings when he was a child. Robert responded affirmatively. "Did you know," asked Seth, "there were literally THREE separate-and-distinct creations, formed by each of you (including the Mother herself), of your Mother?" The idea is important enough, although at the time it was opaque.

There is a possibility in infinity the Mother never existed at all. Or she never got married. Or she had only one son, who never got married. The possibilities are endless. But in our reality, there is one Mother with two sons. So how do all these possibilities turn into our reality?

Possibilities turn into creation. But there must be more to know about this process, and there is. A familiar line from scripture goes something like "It is done unto you as you believe." Even among Biblical Scholars, the wording will be different depending on the translation. But you get the gist ... and "belief" is the operative word.

According to scripture:

> *"Believe that you have received it, and it will be yours." [Mark 11:24]* [16]

---

[16] Crossway Bibles (2011-02-09). The Holy Bible, English Standard Version (Kindle Locations 39758-39760). Good News Publishers/Crossway Books. Kindle Edition.

If one son "believes" the Mother is vengeful, spiteful, and mean, this she will be to him. If the other son "believes" she is nice and kind, she will likewise be that. *One brother is the oldest, and presumably needs to set a good example … at least according to the Mother.* This is how diametrically opposed versions, by different people, of ostensibly the same person or thing happen. Many of her details (height, hair color, etc.) agree, and so scale the ladder from individual into mass consciousness.

In a remarkable way, "Cosmic Mind," through the organ of the brain and individual consciousness, all draw from the same possibility pool. Characteristics of each individual creation will need to be agreed upon for individuals to interact, so in this case certain details about the Mother will be shared. Like her height, hair color, etc. But each is a separate, albeit mostly agreed upon, stand-alone creation of each and every consciousness needing to interact in some way with the Mother, subordinate to an individual's belief.

What is a belief anyway? A belief is a thought that is thought so many times it eventually becomes a conscious thought no more, and is pushed down into the sub-conscious where it operates below the level of normal awareness. Do you think the brothers may have different beliefs about the Mother? Probably, at some point. The important point is: it doesn't matter. Each brother ultimately determines their own experience.

You may think beliefs are only programmed into the brain … but they now reside where they attract similar thoughts, people, things, and situations into their reality, thereby reinforcing themselves. *See, people driving red sports cars really DO drive like a-holes. There goes another one.*

To carry beliefs into the Law of Attraction, there are "good" beliefs and "bad" beliefs. It should be clear which is which. The Law of Attraction further states there are ways to influence your beliefs, and nudge them in a "good" direction. After all, who wants a "bad" job, boss, relationship, health, finances, life (and the list is all-inclusive) if you know better?

"Why would I possibly do *that* (bad thing) to myself" you may wonder? How can you play the game if you don't know the rules? *You have landed on "Jail" again, but cannot collect your two-hundred dollars.* You will do better when you know the rules.

In some psychic circles, others may know, or at least use, "the rules" better. The communication is one-way, and might involve a "reading" given by a person known as a "medium." Some may use tools and become card-readers. Genuine card-readers may use their cards to tap into the Akashic records and give the subject a reading on what the most likely possibilities are, from where the subject is *at that moment in time* on their Roadmap-of-Life.

Astrologers (or Numerologists) may give accurate readings for those living their lives on the Roadmap-of-Life, whether they know it or not. If you are a victim of life coming at you, this reading might be especially valuable. Once one has taken control over their life, the roadmap is subject to conscious change. All life circumstances, including change, would be under the auspices of a specific astrological sign, should you believe in Astrology.

Knowing very little about Astrology, I AM a water sign. *Does anyone not know what sign they are, and what group your sign belongs to?* So, by taking conscious control over my life, changes would probably *not* show up as available to a fire sign. *Although I have been known to order food with a red star next to it in a Chinese restaurant. Talk about FIRE, especially if you eat what you shouldn't have!*

Now that we know programmed beliefs control our experiences, and our reality is proceeding, let's complete the circle and go back to the *Infinite*. We'll go back and use a previous example, while keeping it in our current reality – it's the Wright Brothers and the airplane. Even that example built on other inventions such as the gasoline engine.

The Wright Brothers added their understanding of aerodynamics to airplanes. They had brought an idea from the *Infinite*, and completed it in their reality. Now let's bring their understanding of aerodynamics into the current world of flying, and put all the ideas *back* into the *Infinite*.

It's now decades later, and we have the 747 jumbo-jet. *I don't think passengers are pedaling them or flapping their arms.* Not only does it use a presumably advanced understanding of aerodynamics, *unless you don't care because you had enough to drink at the airport bar,* but also uses thousands of parts, so we'll pick one: copper wire. There are miles of wire in a 747, of every gauge (thickness) needed to control every remote electrical part including control surfaces. Pilots even have a term for it: "fly by wire."

Once upon a time, someone figured out that copper was an efficient conductor of electricity, had other properties like malleability, and you could use different thicknesses. You could also jacket a copper wire to provide insulation from other nearby wires. All these ideas came from the *Infinite*, and somebody developed them into copper wire in our reality.

They are trying to re-open parts of a Copper mine in AK, closed in the 1930s, as a tourist attraction. It was, and still is, the richest deposit of copper ever found. It was closed as a boom in copper expired, and the mine was moved to UT where it exists today. Mining copper at different locations, and all the related activities, are in a reality that includes copper.

The 747 itself was a once just a gleam in somebody's mind, but now fleets of them have collapsed the size of the real world. This represents the complete circle. Ideas come from the *Infinite*, are developed in the real world, and go back again. Now the collapsed size of our world is taken for granted, and has become firmly entrenched in the *Infinite*.

For anyone making their ideas into a reality today, if they need to go somewhere, they might get on a 747. They can get their ticket on the Internet, and money out of an ATM. The circle is complete.

To counter the assumption posed at the beginning of this section, there is creativity or *real* creativity involved in this process, regardless of the how the ego classifies anything. Something has been made visible, real or physical from the *Infinite*, developed in the *Finite*, and re-deposited into the *Infinite*.

Einstein said . . .

Einstein is credited as being one of the great thinkers of the 20th century. He had what might be the most famous equation in history: $E = mc^2$, *supposedly leading to the atom bomb, but what's one little mistake?* Nuclear power, another descendent of this equation, was supposed to make power so plentiful and cheap it was going to be free. Nixon had a saying: "One thousand by two thousand." *Of course, he was a politician with moving lips, so you knew he was lying.*

Nixon meant one-thousand nuclear reactors by the year 2000. We would have *free* power by the year 2000, according to prevalent thinking. Instead of 1000 by 2000, along came Three Mile Island and Jimmy Carter, and the Russians got Chernobyl. People may hate Nixon, but everybody still loves Einstein. *He had such cool hair!*

Let's take a look at Einstein's famous equation: $E = mc^2$, but a slight adjustment is needed for the *Infinite.* First look at the components: "E" (energy) equals "m" (mass or matter or stuff) times "c" (a "very large" constant which equals, in this case, the speed-of-light), which subsequently gets squared. Einstein liked the speed-of-light in his theories, plus it is "quantifiable" in scientific terms. But the important point is the equal sign, in which energy and mass are equated. *For some reason, squaring things is what they did.*

First let's take the "squared" out of the equation because it does not make sense in this context. Now move the "c" to the other side, while changing it to mean "consciousness" instead of a very-large-constant. *The best part is ... the "c" stays!* Now the equation reads Ec = m, OR (read the same way with different words) the product of energy and consciousness is matter aka "stuff." The equation now reads: ec = m and is an equation for the *Infinite* AND the *Finite* – equating energy and stuff via consciousness. *Nixon is "out" … Einstein remains "in."*

Even after Einstein abandoned his childhood religion, he continued with faith. So he didn't abandon his tendencies, only what he termed religion. Regardless of this break, he is credited with saying a lot to bridge the gap between science and religion and said:

- *"Try and penetrate with our limited means the secrets of nature, and you will find that, behind all the discernible laws and connections, there remains something subtle, intangible, and inexplicable. Veneration for this force beyond anything we can comprehend is my religion. To that extent I am, in fact, religious."*
- *"Science without religion is lame. Religion without science is blind."*
- *"The world as we have created it is a process of our thinking. It cannot be changed without changing our thinking."* [17]
- *You can never create nor destroy energy, but it only changes form.*

The last paraphrased quote (from Einstein's First Law of Thermodynamics) makes a good segue into the following discussion. With all this invisible energy permeating everything everywhere (some physicists call it the "unified field") and "Infinite Mind" or "Cosmic Consciousness" (or whatever label you want to attach) also everywhere, what happens when you merge them together?

Energy *does* change form, as Einstein said, and ultimately presents the physical representation of an idea heretofore invisible. In this

[17] Dyer, Serena J.; Dyer, Wayne W. (2014-06-16). Don't Die with Your Music Still in You: My Experience Growing Up with Spiritual Parents (p. 91). Hay House, Inc.. Kindle Edition.

Power of Creation process, going from the *Infinite* to our *Finite* reality occurs in the brain of the observer, and involves energy and "stuff." One can say the *Infinite,* the *Finite,* and the *Power of Creation* have been used together to create stuff, which is now real to us.

In terms of portraying reality, if the world created by our thinking – our reality – includes what might be termed a "problem," the same thinking will only produce more of the same (including the problem). Our thinking must change before experiencing something new, which might include a solution to the problem. So says Einstein.

With Einstein, it wasn't a mutually exclusive proposition as in: either science OR religion, but not both. It seems clear from Einstein's first two quotes above, this man normally labelled a scientist, embraced both. Just because something can't be explained in scientific terms, does not mean it doesn't exist, as explained via the Roadmap-of-Life analogy. *Remember Paris?* Even so, science will keep trying to "prove" how an idea becomes physical. Science will keep trying to prove it, measure it, and predict it via equations. *Such is my prediction.*

Trying to measure an idea sounds like one of those oxymoronic *(with the emphasis on moron)* things. How did the initial idea of a wireless phone morph into today's iPhone? You could probably quantify the manufacturing costs, and other items associated with each stage in the evolution of the wireless phone, but let me know when you can "measure" an idea. Here's yet *another* prediction: there will even be more ideas becoming visible!

In our reality, the first law of thermodynamics tells us energy, or matter, can be changed back and forth, but energy itself cannot be created nor destroyed. Although a chemical change results in a new substance, the total weight of the ingredients involved remains the same. In mathematical terms Einstein revealed mass and energy are equivalent to each other — when one is "destroyed" the other is "created." [18]

There was this Sunday talk ("sermon" if you prefer the older religious term) where the speaker quoted another well-known Pastor ("coach" if you like newer terms) whereby if you did not have at least twenty-five goals going, you are wasting your life.

I can easily get 25 things going at once, where #26 would have pushed one of the previous off the conga line, like a game of musical chairs. Continually starting new things is fun, so my life is complete. According to the Roadmap-of-Life, I wouldn't know where I was; being on 25 roads at the same time indicates a GPS problem!

Einstein said

"work on one thing at a time."

---

[18] Roberts, Jane (2011-09-30). The Nature of Personal Reality: Specific, Practical Techniques for Solving Everyday Problems and Enriching the Life You Know (A Seth Book) (Kindle Locations 2927-2931). Amber-Allen Publishing. Kindle Edition.

Let's Invent Something

A long time ago, good-ol' square-glasses Ben Franklin *(the glasses will be back in fashion soon)* went out flying a kite in a thunderstorm with a key attached to the string for some reason ... you're familiar with the image. *As the warning legalese might say in fine print on the bottom of your TV screen: "Trained thunderstorm kite-flyer. Do not attempt." What they always leave out is: "moron." Of course, you may not buy the car that is flying over things if idiot lawyers called you a moron. They used to call it "thinning the herd."*

Ben was understanding more about the nature of electricity. Ultimately what he was doing was "inventing" the lightning rod, to protect anything using it from lightning, including tall buildings. *The lightning rod is quite literally to be thanked for tall buildings.*

Many will *not* be familiar with this part of the story: after Ben had his "proof of concept," he made a lightning rod but refused to patent it, saying it was too important to be limited in use to those who would pay a patent royalty, or have someone make money from it. *Such was life back in those days.*

Today, our understanding of electricity has been refined to encompass toasters, TVs, and light-bulbs, etc. All these items include aspects of electricity, with many using knowledge of other things, including smaller and smaller electrical components. Now smart phones would be the size of the Empire State Building without the accompanying understanding of electronics and the miniaturization of components. *And the Empire State Building itself would not exist without lightning rods.*

Thank goodness *(there's another "small-g" word to use instead of "[the big G-Man]")* electrical, electronic, and other types of engineers understand enough about what they do to "invent" whatever it is. Just tell me how to turn it on. Other instructions are supposedly learned from the manual, *the reading of which, like asking for directions, real men don't do. Google is great for learning stuff without ever reading a manual written by lawyers. Did you ever wonder why you have to "agree" to all the legalese before proceeding on-line?*

Back to square-glasses Ben. He never patented the lightning rod, nor did he ever claim to invent electricity. Electricity (and lightning) was always there, and Ben only sought to understand it better. *Lightning was around even before kites.* Now our understanding of electricity and electronics has proceeded to involve smart-phones.

Before going any farther, know no-one "invents" anything any more than Ben "invented" electricity, although it is currently popular to claim to have invented something. It not only takes time and effort to understand something better, but one must have the idea to do so – hence patents, copyrights, trademarks, etc. were invented by lawyers.

Electricity was around "forever" before Ben, and there will be even more inventions to come out of understanding electricity even better or smaller. In fact, computers are now being used to design themselves, hence a piggy-backing effect. *Inventions are scary to non-priests.*

Did you know there was once a patent office official who resigned, predicting the patent office would go out of existence, because everything worthwhile had already been invented? Did you know (even more useless trivia) the story was tracked down and is false? But it seems so believable with what we "know" about government.

More non-trivial information about Patents. *Every* possibility is contained within the *Infinite*, along with energy which changes form, thereby making the idea visible in our reality. Can you think of anything that leaves out? *BTW, Ben never patented anything, and he's on our money!*

So the question becomes: Does anyone ever "invent" anything, or simply discover how to use something already there? The question becomes a little harder when something like a board game ("intellectual property") is considered, so let's use one most already know: ***Monopoly.***

In this example, "intellectual property" *is* valuable. The "idea" for ***Monopoly***, as well as what would be considered other "creative" endeavors of all types (paintings, poems, music, along with all other "art") by our definition must come from the *Infinite*. After merging with energy that subsequently changes form, the idea then becomes visible in our reality. The idea passes through whatever levels of mass consciousness might be involved, and continues on to the individual's consciousness who has developed the idea. Someone trained as an artist of some type connects with infinity, and thereby brings the work-of-art into existence. The patenting, or copyright, *et al* process gives it $$$ value.

Someone claims to have invented ***Monopoly***. Others made a painting, poem, or piece of music. Even though people are people in our reality and apparently will always be stealing something, a claim of authorship that involves something real seems more provable than claims of ownership of something less tangible. *Lawyers keep busy proving people did what they say, and the courts decide who stole whatever from whom and how much it's worth. Lawyers get a third regardless.*

Bringing us to the point of *who* actually did <whatever> <whenever>. If all possibilities (ideas) reside in the *Infinite*, who's to say who first tapped into it and came up with the idea? Whoever filed for the patent or copyright first, our Legal (not Spiritual) Law says, in our reality of linear time. A lot of people come up with the same idea at once. Someone files for a patent first in linear time and thereby gets "The Law" on their side. *BTW, if everything is subservient to Spiritual Law, then Legal Law must be subservient to Spiritual Law too, right?*

You cannot patent anything already in production, whether or not it already has a patent associated with it. Nor can you just knock-it-off, even though people do. People are people. What you *can* do is improve upon it, patent the improvement, and maybe sell the improvement back to the original patent-holder. You have then joined the ranks of patent-holders, doing whatever they do, with their lawyers *(who always get one-third)*. The improvement, along with the original idea, came from the *Infinite. If you're Christian, or even if you're not, you know most lawyers came from Hell.*

What *is* important: the idea for the patent or copyright came from somewhere, and in our reality, is given value through developing it – which takes time and effort. It's less the idea than the process of developing it that is patentable or valuable.

Somehow a "savant" has by-passed the time and effort spent in training for whatever they do, whether it be solving equations or playing the piano. They have provided and thereby *proved by demonstration* a direct link to the *Infinite.* Who knows if the mental effort of a savant can be duplicated, but in today's world of brain-scan MRIs, scientists will keep trying.

And so continues the evolution of consciousness.

Affirmations and Meditation

There are many, many spiritual disciplines, some more organized than others. *Some are older, some more Eastern, some more Western, some more disciplined, some more organized, while some have their own town.* The most organized spiritual disciplines being around the longest are often labelled religions.

Most religions offer a rational explanation, claiming to know (and offer to teach, or act as a go-between *for a small donation or, alternatively, everything you own*) how to get from the *Infinite* to the *Finite* reality of our life. Some religions get involved with other areas considered "morality." Regardless of how organized, there are some aspects they all have in common, if you take a step back and forget whatever different words they attribute to the same practices.

The first shared practice is most commonly known in today's parlance as affirmations. You may know how affirmations are supposed to be formed: present tense, self-directed, and positive. A good example would be "I AM rich." I generally capitalize "I AM" to remind myself of the power of the "I AM" statement – automatically making what follows it true, unless cancelled by something else.

> *How we finish the sentence that begins with "I [AM]" makes all the difference in the life we create for ourselves and how close or far away we are from the part of us that is [the big G-man.]* [19]

---

[19] Dyer, Wayne W.; Tracy, Kristina (2012-03-01). I Am: Why Two Little Words Mean So Much (Kindle Locations 30-31). Hay House. Kindle Edition.

Use an affirmation like "I am a klutz" at your own peril. It may seem self-deprecating and funny, but it's not positive. And it *will* attract supporting experiences.

In some ancient religions, verbalizing the equivalent of "I AM" was prohibited. In Judaism, the most accepted terminology was "I am that I am" in their language, thereby attaching words to [the big G-Man], which thereby alluded to the *Infinite*. Remember, attaching words to anything *Infinite* only alludes to it, and makes it *Finite* so you can "understand" and talk about it. Attaching words may have given the prohibition.

What you are also doing in the "I AM" declaration is invoking the creative power of the mind, related to yourself, via the *Power of Creation*. When you make the affirmation "I AM rich," if you accept the statement as true, then so be it, as long as you do not simultaneously invoke "but" which completely cancels the original affirmation. Like language, using a "but" effectively cancels anything before it. *As in "I like your $200 hairstyle, but it makes you look like your mother." You get the drift, BUT maybe you don't!*

If you are already wealthy, you are probably *not* doing the "I AM rich" affirmation, although you may have done a similar one to get that way. Now maybe you are doing other affirmations related to health or relationships.

Most likely a financially affluent person, using an "I AM healthy" affirmation, is somehow invoking the "but" cancellation, this time using health, or he or she would already have good health. This is why they continue to have health problems.

If he or she were to affirm the wealth they already have, no caveat would be simultaneously generated to cancel the statement, and it is already true anyway. Remember, your reality already completely and accurately reflects your mind. You don't change the reflection by banging on the mirror. *A fun-house has lots of mirrors. That's why it's fun.*

Instead, if you are using affirmations like "I AM prosperous" (prosperity embraces more than just financial rich-ness, but also other aspects like health, relationships, job, boss, etc.) If you include these other issues along with prosperity and also trigger the "but" cancellation, you will stay stuck right where you are.

The "but" cancellation affects our prosperity affirmations of whatever type: weight loss or gain (right and perfect body), health, relationships, and myriads of other goals. Learning about goal setting comes from lots of sources including business: set a specific, measurable goal and a time-frame for its completion. In this sense, it is the same for spirituality – but in the spiritual version, you must be especially careful *not* to invoke the "but" cancellation.

In business, goals are often set by one's boss, so it doesn't matter if the goal invokes any other cancellation, like "but I need to see my family!" *In fact, it is very likely to invoke "But you're an a-hole!" Probably the same sentiment he or she had when the goal was handed to them.* But *(Butt crack, so to speak)* most likely, they are not operating in the realm of the spiritual. All the boss has to do is make the employees work overtime to accomplish a goal set further above, so the boss gets their promotion and raise. *The boss apparently affirmed: "I am rich (BUT you're not!)" The boss probably drives a red sports-car.*

Looking at the spiritual – not business – world, the goal gets implanted as realistic in our brain, while you are careful NOT to mentally invoke the "but" factor. There is no boss involved, just yourself. *If you refer to yourself as an "a-hole," well that's a whole (fun pun) 'nother discussion for another time! If you do so, perhaps your first affirmation may be to stop referring to yourself in such a manner by a certain time. Or else go on the Dr. Phil show.*

In the first affirmation example "I AM rich," is there anything specific and measurable about it, and a certain time-frame?

Being rich means living beyond the next pay-check to some, and something else to others. And when is it to be accomplished by? By the end of this year? *By the time you're looking at grass from the other side (or some other euphemism by which you refer to death)?* Make sure to use measureable specificity and a time-frame.

Once again, "I AM" invokes a principle of seeing yourself as Creation itself – the equivalent phrase is not even to be uttered in some ancient religions. So here I capitalize "I AM," and give pause before I utter the words "I AM" before *anything*, and look carefully at what follows.

How many people would choose as an affirmation, "I AM <something>," where the <something> is not positive? Have you remembered to set a measurable goal in a certain time frame? So you will be, what, broke, by a certain date? *Well, I guess if you were currently worse-than-broke (in debt), being just broke by a certain date might be a step up.*

Here's an important point: you cannot mention "debt" in an affirmation, whether it be less or none or whatever, without invoking the concept of "debt" itself.

The founder of Religious Science (Science of Mind) Ernest Holmes said many times

> *"turn completely away from the problem."*

By this statement, and in this example, he would mean NOT mentioning "debt" in any manner, so as not to affirm the idea of debt – so don't do it.

Using the term "free and clear" in affirmations halfway refers to the idea of debt (none). Money in the bank does not include any thoughts of debt. So by now your affirmation may be "I have $10,000 in the bank by 1/1/<some year>." If you still feel a cancellation affixed to the affirmation, you might change the amount to $1,000 or even $100, and modify the time-frame.

Words are used by the rational / *Finite* side of the brain. Once you make a believable affirmation (some suggest writing it down a specific number of times EVERY DAY) you have set the wheels of the Universe in motion, which sets about fulfilling your order, complete with synchronicity provided by the *Infinite*.

Some disciplines suggest never looking at the results, like pulling up a plant to see if it is growing. Others say keep looking to get positive feedback, like keep stepping on the bathroom scale. Religious Science says keep doing it until it is done, meaning it has been accomplished in mind – your reality will reflect it.

If you want to have a certain result by a certain time, how can you possibly achieve it if you never look at it, you may ask? Well, a year after achieving a goal, one may say it is done, assuming you had achieved the goal. You probably had also stopped (best if you had forgotten about) doing an affirmation *toward* achieving the goal. You may bring it to mind – briefly – before stating "I'll never do *that* again!" Quickly forget it.

Working backward into organized religions we see what they have is similar. Religions don't have affirmations, but they do have what they call prayer, so let's start there. The religious person is probably praying to somebody or something. *If your Deity has a human form, perhaps it resembles a long-bearded Charlton Heston sitting on a cloud arbitrarily hurling lightning bolts in your direction. Some consider [the big G-Man] as not only Charlton Heston sitting on his cloud, but everything else also.* But no matter who or what you think you are praying *to*, do you actually think you are going to change the Deities mind, especially about your little human affair? *You may actually pray you are going to convince Charlton not to hurl a lightning bolt in your direction today. Perhaps if you grit your teeth, turn blue in the face and pray hard enough, you may get what you are praying for.*

When one examines religious prayer, you may think you are praying to somebody. But, at the root of your prayer, you are praying to *both* yourself and [the big G-Man] via both sides of your brain; you are planting a suggestion in your own mind, the same as the affirmation described above. Prayer can come complete with the "but" cancellation, so be-in-tune to your prayer. *So if you are praying to Charlton not to hurl a lightning bolt in you direction, yet have the "but" feeling in there, guess what? Charlton might be hurling some lightning bolts in your direction. You may NOT want to put up your umbrella on the golf course.*

If you are praying for health, or even better yet for someone else's health (consciousness is non-local i.e. everywhere) and have a belief in the cure mixed in, then the subject can "touch the hem of His garment" and effect health. You haven't really convinced anybody of anything, other than planted a seed in consciousness, which starts growing. *Don't dig-it-up to see if it's growing.* Such is how prayer and affirmations are similar, and work – or not. Prayer has belief, as do affirmations, but beware! Both can have the "but" cancellation attached if you're not careful.

Prayers or affirmations are us addressing Creation; whereby intuition, gut-feelings, synchronicity, and co-incidences are Creation answering back. Such is where the practice of meditation comes in. Before delving into specific varieties of meditation, they all have one purpose: to quiet the "monkey mind" (incessant internal jibber-jabber). Meditation also gives a chance for the *Infinite* to get a word in edgewise, although in supreme irony, there can be no words. As a side benefit, a practice of meditation gives us a little peace-of-mind, or a break from the internal dialog.

The easiest meditation, although it may not be a meditation *per se* but does connect you more with your spirit (your higher self), can be practiced anywhere at any time. You will notice when you are tense, your breathing is shallow. The easiest way to fix this is by deep breathing. You do not have to breathe in through your nose and out through your mouth, hold it for a specific count, nor breathe in a certain way – just breathe deeply. It can be closed-eyed or open-eyed – it doesn't matter. Just breathe deeply. You can use it any time … *if need be, excuse yourself for a moment. OK, go to the can for [the big G-man] sake!*

One of the open-eyed, stay present, meditations from **Zen Driving**, involves a very-safe method of driving. You'll have to read the book to find out more. When practiced, it shuts off the words by flooding the consciousness. One of the major goals from the Carlos Castaneda **Don Juan series**, similarly involves shutting down the chatter. Many of these, too, are practiced open-eyed, and ultimately shut down words. The **Don Juan series** uses the term "internal dialog," and the shutting down of it is instrumental. Since people only think in the *Finite* using words, minimizing words would seemingly place us closer to the *Infinite*.

Other meditations are closed-eyed. They may have a mantra attached, like "Om" (one of the easiest and most common) or one of the supposedly secret mantras they assign to you in TM. Meditations may involve focusing your attention on your breath, or heartbeat. Some of those focusing on the breath would be more involved than the simple one listed above. If you are focusing on your heartbeat, the meditation may have you feel the blood flowing from your heart and going to nourish different parts of your body.

There are guided aural (sound) meditations, mostly closed-eyed, maybe involving your chakras, travelling to a meadow, or other more hypnotic techniques. In others, you feel your consciousness expanding, eventually to encompass beyond yourself, to the sun, to the solar system, to the galaxy, and eventually the entire Universe.

Since now technologies measure brain wave frequencies, the most direct methods of programming or *re*-programming the sub-conscious come at the lower frequencies, where the least "interference" from the conscious level occurs. This occurs naturally after birth, with almost no conscious involvement through age two. Then we get more involved through age eight, after which our consciousness takes over and filters what gets through to our sub-conscious as we learn the rules-of-life. Filtering happens via already implanted beliefs (aka programming), so watch out for those first two years! In later life, perceptions are *provided* and filtered to match our consciousness, whenever and however it has been programmed.

One of the goals of meditation is to slow our consciousness down to a level more representative of an earlier chronological age, where suggestions can be re-programmed into our sub-conscious with the least interference. Once the subject is back to normal consciousness, the "but" factor will be involved in what behavior the trigger will elicit. So the subject will probably not walk and quack like the *Aflac* duck if he normally wouldn't.

It has been stated one of the goals of meditation is to calm down our "monkey mind" whereby words are not so dominant. Calming down the left side of the brain can be measured by brain wave frequency. A side benefit: the less words going round-and-round in our brain, the more peace-of-mind. To that extent, a direct channel to the *Infinite* is opened.

This section is finished by mentioning the feeling of worthiness, or more correctly, the *lack* thereof. There is a whole school of thought dictating *all* the problems that make a mental discipline NOT work can be boiled down to one problem – our own feeling of *lack* of worthiness. Even with the best of intentions, parents go down the check-out line with the two-year-old in the shopping cart seat, saying "No" to everything the young-un wants to grab … you've probably witnessed this. In the wide-open programming stage the two-year-old is in, how can the child come away from the experience *not* having an unworthy feeling?

With all respect due to the parents of any two-year-old, how could the parents do anything differently? Should you give the child everything he or she wants? (There are some "disciplines" suggesting this.) *Leave the kid in the car with the dog, buckled in his car seat. Make sure the windows are cracked to avoid animal endangerment charges! Otherwise they might start screaming or barking in the supermarket. (Just jesting for those parents without any sense of humor whatsoever.)*

Do *not* make any affirmations or prayers invoking the "but" clause negatively, and work on feelings of unworthy-ness. Remember, your life is a complete and accurate reflection of what you have going on in your mind.

If you want, BUT only if you want, you can:

> *"Change your mind – change your life"*

The Anatomy of a Belief

Back in the time of scripture, sentiments like "It is done unto you as you believe" were coined, even though no-one may have specifically defined what a belief was. You simply knew it to be so, and there it was: the belief *was* the belief itself. *Tell me that doesn't bend your logical brain. Plus they changed "you" into "ye" to make sure you (ye) knowed ye was a-readin' scripture.*

At one time, knowing the sun will rise tomorrow when it is night-time, went from superstition (with a polygamous Sun God) to belief. Before flat-earth times, the belief that "the sun will continue to rise" was both the subject of, and the belief, itself. By flat-earth times, the belief the sun will rise tomorrow had been upgraded to a knowing. Today we can scientifically "prove" it via pictures from above the earth, and the earth's rate-of-rotation, etc. but it was not always so.

Winter precedes Spring, and then comes Summer, Fall and back to Winter. There was a fallow time, a planting time, a growing season, harvest, and back to fallow. Ancient monuments like Stonehenge were erected to give seasons timing, so one could plan to plant and harvest accordingly, via the Solstices. Holidays (or "Holy Days") were celebrated after Winter Solstice, when the celebrators knew the days would be getting longer again, and the seasons would continue. At some point a belief, upgraded to a knowing, involved the seasons.

These ancient cycles go beyond a superstition, to the belief they will keep happening (we don't consciously think of them), to an even stronger knowing. *In the same manner, no-one has to think about gravity unless you're ready to jump off something, out of something (as in an airplane, if you like sky-diving) or are mountain climbing.*

There are many more "man-made" beliefs (not "facts" of nature) going on, that turn into a knowing. And beliefs form our reality, like "The World is a Cruel Place" or "The World is a Kind, Gentle, and Supportive Place." If anyone is harboring one of these mutually exclusive beliefs, they *will* get the circumstances. Getting the belief then reinforces it, and it will continue to attract the same result, and around and around until it eventually becomes a knowing. If something opposite comes along, it will be seen as a quirk and ignored, if the opposite perception enters a person's consciousness at all.

So how did it get this way? Modern technology lends us a hand. Through the electro-encephalogram (EEG), brain wave frequency of an individual's brain is measured. Different levels are classified as follows:

- Delta
  - Frequency 0.5 – 4 cycles / second
  - Representative of:
    - Children through age 2
    - Deep Sleep
- Theta
  - Frequency 4 - 8 cycles / second
  - Representative of:
    - Children ages 3 - 6
    - Trance, Imagination
    - Meditation
- Alpha
  - Frequency 8 - 13 cycles / second
  - Representative of:
    - Children ages 7 - 8
    - Occurs naturally with closed eyes
- Beta
  - Low Beta Frequency 13 - 15 cycles / second
  - Medium Beta Frequency 16 - 22 cycles / second

- o High Beta Frequency 22 - 50 cycles / second
- o Fight-or-Flight (or freeze)
- o Representative of:
  - • Children ages 9 – 12 and beyond; adults
  - • Waking state
- • Gamma
  - o A newly-discovered state
  - o Representative of gurus in elevated consciousness

Our brain unconditionally accepts all perceptions a child would have through age two (Delta). Then our consciousness starts to develop, and we choose our beliefs a little more selectively up to about age six (Theta) *but the stage has been set!* In the later phases of this state, the child can easily remain in an imaginary state for a long period, when they are determining the rules-of-life – it's easier to play the game when you know the rules!

Then the reasoning conscious takes over completely, filters what it perceives, and allows into the conscious only what it approves of between ages seven and eight (Alpha). It is important to note that, for an adult in the Beta state, merely closing the eyes will move one into the Alpha state.

After the child's brain comes into adult maturity, the waking state is represented by the three different Beta levels; the highest vibration in the Beta state is representative of the "fight-or-flight" level. A newly discovered frequency is Gamma, only observed in meditating individuals in elevated consciousness. [20]

Growing up, "ideas" have selectively entered our consciousness. Up through age two, as infants, we can't make our own choices … so the ideas our parents or caregivers provide are it. Hopefully they are mostly positive, but nobody's perfect!

---

[20] Dispenza, Joe (2012-02-15). Breaking the Habit of Being Yourself: How to Lose Your Mind and Create a New One (p. 185-8). Hay House. Kindle Edition.

At the next stage, to about age six, we are able to start filtering ourselves what will – and won't – get into our conscious. Our caregivers provide the guidance for what gets into our consciousness … more at the beginning. Then, between ages five and six, as a growing child we are now half consciousness internal and half external, in order to figure out what the rules of existing are. In the later Theta state, the child is also able to exist in an imaginary state interminably.

Beyond age eight, the child starts to mature into adult-hood as evidenced by his brain wave frequencies which have now entered the different Beta states. The highest beta level is sometimes known as the "fight-or-flight" level (some use "fight, flight, or freeze"), which is useful when confronted with an actual situation like an imminent bear attack. Remaining in the fight-or-flight state too long results in the stress our culture is so familiar with.

Most of our programming occurs in childhood, while mostly defenseless against it. Contrary perceptions are filtered out and never enter our consciousness. Many people swear they will never do <whatever their parents did> but ultimately do so – they have had their parents beliefs programmed in. Coherent thoughts come in through our filters at any time and are thought over-and-over, to be ultimately programmed as beliefs and pushed out of our conscious awareness into the *sub*-conscious (*un*-conscious implies consciousness is never to be re-attained).

Let's review what a belief actually is. A belief is a thought that is thought so many times over and over it becomes automatic. Our filtering system usually doesn't even allow in contrary perceptions. Programming moves the belief down into our sub-conscious. An even stronger belief is termed a knowing.

When you "know" something is true, you thereby know it to be a *fact*. No two ways about it. How many things do you know to be so? Gravity and linear time are a *fact*. (Both are considered elements of, or agreements in, mass consciousness.) Do you know one or the other of "The World is a Cruel Place" or "The World is a Kind, Gentle, and Supportive Place" to be a *fact*? They are mutually exclusive, so you cannot select both. How many knowings are given us courtesy of our caregivers or religion or school programming? Hint: most of 'em!

It's also important to realize the chances of over-riding programming via reason and intellect is small. Most people wind up doing what their parents did, regardless of what they "think" about it. To use what most will consider a positive example, adult children keep celebrating Christmas and other Christian holidays, while taking their own children to Mass (and raising the children as Catholic) even if they have "thought" better of it themselves. They were programmed Catholic by their parents, whose parents were programmed Catholic by their parents, and so on, and so on. *The Christmas Tree industry depends on Christians following the Holiday traditions, as does the Hallmark Greeting Card Company.*

There is a verse in Scripture that says something like

"The Sins of the Father are visited upon the Son."

This would include the Christian Father / Son thing, accordingly ...

First comes a re-definition of the word "sin" which is not as generally known, but is actually an ancient archery term meaning "missing the mark." So the *Father* misses the mark, and "visits" (passes down) missing the mark to his *Son* (programs the son or daughter accordingly), who pass the programming down to their kids and so on, and so on. The *Infinite* (Father) misses the mark while passing down programming to the *Finite* (his Son).

The definition of "meme" (created by the biologist Richard Dawkins, pronounced 'meem') tells us a meme is "a unit of cultural transmission, or a unit of imitation" and is meant to evoke the idea of a gene. If handing negative memes down to future generations is not desirable, saying things to our children should be examined (i.e. what the *Father* visits to the *Son*). Our kids will end up believing our memes, and the result is entire generations with limited beliefs about life. They'll have expectations before they're old enough to come to conclusions on their own. [21]

Our own brain wave frequency levels (by using meditation, hypnosis and other well defined techniques) can now be selected in order to most effectively *re*-program our thoughts which ultimately become our beliefs. It is *not* important to know the source of the initial thought. What *is* important is knowing which frequency is most effective in *re*-programming the belief, and have some method for getting there.

An important note is in order. Some aberrant behavior on my part was not "understood" until:

1) Self-hypnosis discovered the origin of one behavior (knowing nothing about brain wave frequencies at the time), and
2) An image from early childhood "floated" into my awareness about the other.

So the initial thought or experience *remains* to control our behavior. These particular experiences come from my less-than-two-years-old arena, and will never be "proven."

A word about TM. The meditation technique employed by Transcendental Meditation (TM) uses a closed-eye state (automatically switching the subject to an Alpha state) with a customized mantra, while letting invading thoughts gently go, while returning to the mantra. Successful usage of the TM technique would switch the subject into the Theta state. TM, as I

---

[21] Dyer, Serena J.; Dyer, Wayne W. (2014-06-16). Don't Die with Your Music Still in You: My Experience Growing Up with Spiritual Parents (p. 95-6). Hay House, Inc. Kindle Edition.

learned it, does not go beyond meditation to replace certain beliefs *or world peace would be upon us.*

Meditation provides many techniques used to change the frequency of a subject from a waking state (Beta, possibly the high vibration "fight-or-flight" level) to a receptive Theta level. Besides making the brain or sub-conscious more receptive to suggestion (as in Hypnosis) where *re*-programing already existing beliefs, meditation will calm the subject down and is relatively easy, although doing it is a discipline *(but easier than working out).*

Let us now assume the subject is in a receptive Theta brain wave frequency state. There are many meditation techniques one uses to get there, and they are relatively easy, but they do require a certain discipline i.e. it is suggested to set aside a certain place and time to perform your meditation and attain this state. So now what does the meditator do?

There are many audio hypnotic suggestion (i.e. MP3) files, as well as other techniques (some are waking and open-eyed, some sleeping) available, used to *re*-program the beliefs buried way down in the sub-conscious. If you use your meditation and replacement technique enough, eventually the hidden belief will be replaced with a new one, and *voila!* your new reality comes automatically with your new belief. But you may never actually recognize it unless you are extremely conscious.

Remember, there are as many techniques available as there are cookbooks giving different ways to cook a roast. Some suggest using a quiet, undisturbed spot to listen to MP3 suggestions through headphones, which may be closest to actual (or self-) hypnosis. Others would have you listen to suggestions through computer speakers in the background while going about your normal day. Some use night-time suggestions, which may be effective since sometimes you are in the Delta or Deep Sleep state, and may use an under-the-pillow speaker.

Whichever meditation and / or *re*-programming technique you may use (you can use a combination of them) just keep doing it or them until a change shows up.

An oft-repeated motto (from Religious Science) drifts to the forefront of my consciousness:

> *"Change your mind – change your life"* [22]

---

[22] Holmes, Ernest (2011-01-10). The Science of Mind - Complete Unedited Original Edition (Kindle Locations 287-289). Peerless Communications. Kindle Edition.

Mass Consciousness

On the one hand, you have "Infinite Mind," "Cosmic Consciousness" or whatever other label you may want to attach ... *I'm still not going to use the overused label* ... it is called the *Infinite* here. On literally the other hand, you have the *Finite* some call reality. The process going from one to the other is labelled the *Power of Creation*, sometimes called life. You would certainly consider what is in-between your hands as your very own life.

Depending on how literal you want to be with "hand," for right-handers you could have right-brain on your left hand, and left-brain on your right hand, going from *Infinite* to *Finite*, invisible to visible, non-physical to physical. Be that as it may, your hands are ultimately attached to you.

In the middle of this *handy* continuum are all the other mass or shared consciousness's in operation. All the programming and filters controlling your individual reality, including mass consciousness, are already in effect. From the bottom-up to the top-down, your reality has already been determined by your programming, which includes all levels of consciousness.

There are those that believe everything *has* consciousness, and others believe everything is the *result of* consciousness. It might just be semantics, but it might be more. A scientist said in an interview, everything in the Universe *has* consciousness. If he is reading this, he might have meant everything is a *result of* consciousness.

People believing everything *has* consciousness have produced works that use a term like "Gaia" to describe the consciousness of the Earth, or of Mother Earth herself. Have you noticed the causation in a term? Does "*It is done unto you as you believe*" give any hints? Therefore you get what you believe! More to the point, you get what you really are. If you truly believe the Earth *has* consciousness, you got it! You *are* your consciousness.

Here we state everything is the *result of* consciousness. If one were to believe everything *has* consciousness, wouldn't that belief be a *result of* consciousness anyway? *I'm sure a student of logic could have a field day with that!*

Let's continue by examining some of the levels of mass consciousness falling between the *Infinite* and the *Finite*. In an argument used elsewhere for another purpose, anyone is challenged to "show me where any line is," but this time it's between this-and-that mass consciousness. Hint: there aren't any lines, except as someone put them in who was assigned to draw boundaries around certain classifications.

The left-brain loves to divide and classify, thereby fitting and sub-dividing everything into its rational scheme. But the truth is, there is no dividing line between this-and-that mass consciousness except as arbitrarily drawn to satisfy the left-brain, which gives us all the separation from anything and everything else the rational ego-bearing left-brain wants.

This is in human consciousness, and *that* is in cultural consciousness, one is prone to say. What if it's in both? If it is "categorized" as mass consciousness, but is in neither of the above, then it must be in another category, right? *"WRONG" McLaughlin is prone to yell.* Male consciousness? Female consciousness? None of the above? Either of the above? All of the above?

If a Venn diagram for consciousness were to be drawn, with circles for "M" and "F," they would be contained within a circle for "Human," and the "M" and "F" circles might overlap into consciousness for other species *(People study doGs ([the big G-word spelled backwards]) to determine their consciousness by how they "smile" or wag their tails.)*

Human consciousness would fall inside Mother Earth consciousness if you felt everything had consciousness, wouldn't it? But if you feel that everything is a result of consciousness, then the reverse would hold true, right? How about if you believe human consciousness lingers, as in an afterlife envisioned by some religions? Or consciousness of all types is independent of physicality? *Our Venn diagram now has so many circles on it to be almost black, with a little white still showing here-and-there!*

Wouldn't it just be easier to draw a line representing infinite consciousness at one end, and personal consciousness at the other? All other types of consciousness are represented by different points on the continuum in-between the ends. If you want to classify the points as "mass consciousness" of one-type-or-another, go ahead – it depends on how your left-brain ego categorizing function is feeling that day.

When we are all-the-way to the infinite end-of-the-line, *or* are all-the-way at the other end-of-the-line using a name of your choosing to describe yourself, is well defined. "Cosmic Consciousness," "All That Is," "[the big G-Man]," might be labels for the infinite end, and all-the-way on the other end labels such as "Individual Consciousness," "My Reality" *(sounds like something dreamed up for a computer folder)*, or "Me" (fill-in-your-name-here) might be used. *To paraphrase the commercial: "Classify all you want … we'll make more."*

Remember, just because there are an extremely large number of items does not make something infinite. If it's visible, it's not infinite, or else the Universe would be full-of-it. Like the grains of sand in every desert, on all the beaches, and in every ocean — you could still theoretically count them. *Maybe it would be "beach consciousness."*

If grains of sand were visible *and* infinite, there would be nothing *but* grains of sand everywhere in everything. *Some of you may feel that way after coming back from the beach.* Consciousness is invisible and everywhere, and everything visible is a *result of* it, might be inferred from the quote in scripture. *But brains with individual consciousness are visible, right?*

So for something to be infinite, it would have to be everywhere-at-once (omnipresent). Further, no matter how many times it is divided or multiplied, you wind up with the same thing. Let's take the idea of possibilities. Go ahead and multiply or divide it by anything – you still wind up with possibilities. How about the silence which some call the voice of [the big G-Man]? The same thing happens with the multiplying or dividing exercise – the result is still silence. [23]

Let's not forget one of the other infinite components – energy – which when merged with consciousness, gives us the physical reality we know. This would be the Law of Attraction in action. But since this section is about consciousness, let's forget energy. But before we do, just remember what the product of energy and consciousness equals (ec = m). Hint: stuff.

---

[23] Dyer, Dr. Wayne W. (2012-12-03). Getting In the Gap: Making Conscious Contact with God Through Meditation (p. 6). Hay House. Kindle Edition.

Made in the Image and Likeness

One of the more famous lines from scripture reads something like "Man was Created in the Image and Likeness of [there's that big G-Man again]." If one substitutes the word "Creation," or "All That Is" for [that pesky G-Man], such a sentiment would still make sense, but without the ability to be turned around by Man or Woman him-or-herself. *Listen up women ... even though [the big G-Man] was a man in the movies, you don't get completely off-the-hook for turning things around backwards!*

In the unique way that seems to be the essence of humanity today, this pearl of wisdom was turned 180 degrees around and made "[The big G-Man] was Created in the Image and Likeness of Man." Therefore if Man *(or Woman)* was jealous, vengeful, spiteful, and angry, so too must be [the big G-Man]. In such a manner [the big G-Man] is created in the image and likeness of Man. Of course he would look human, and we'd call Him "Him." There is still an essential difference in the order of who was formed from what and when.

It doesn't matter if Man has some good characteristics, because for many the image remains of [the big G-Man] looking like Charlton Heston, with a long flowing beard, sitting on his cloud ready to hurl lightning-bolts down on evil-doers. Decisions by Him turned out fairly arbitrarily, predicated on what kind of a day He was having. *This is why [the big G-Man] is given a male persona. There was a time in history when Feds were referred to as "G-men," but they didn't have [the big G-Man] in mind. At the time, "G" stood for government, but now G-men are alphabet boys with three letters (i.e. EPA, IRS, etc.) people love to hate.*

Women are generally thought to have nicer characteristics, like loving, forgiving, and kind, which is another reason why [the big

G-Man] is given a male persona. In Judaism (The Old Testament), [the big G-Man] was supposed to be nasty, and the religion itself is matriarchal. In Christianity, Jesus was supposed to be the kind, loving one. Many Christians consider Jesus to be [the big G-Man] Himself and not just his Son, plus the resultant religion is patriarchal.

Let's re-write the famous line from scripture using some new words, so now it reads "Man was created in the Image and Likeness of Creation." If one turns it around backwards to read "Creation is created in the Image and Likeness of Man" it still makes sense. Since creation itself (i.e. the Universe) cannot be full of nothing *but* men (and women), "Image and Likeness" must refer to the idea of what has been created.

Now man or woman is both responsible – and accountable – for his or her own creation, by using the power each individual inherently has (aka their consciousness). One's *personal* consciousness is equated with their physical body and resides in their brain, while mass consciousness is non-local i.e. everywhere.

With even more appropriate wording, the saying is now: "Reality is created by the power inherently within Mankind." What power might that be? Mankind's own individual perception formed by beliefs and consciousness. The saying has now ultimately become: "The Universe is created by the brain of man or woman." *Something must have gotten lost in the translation.*

If each of us forms our own reality, then we personally create our very own Universe ... which is *our* part of creation (if one is to use a quasi-religious term).

Religion into Science into Quantum Physics

There was a time when religions, starting with the first major Western monotheistic religion, Judaism (and presumably previous Eastern religions) had no weights, measures, and equations. *Because the church was the ruling body, there were always enough bushels to measure a 10% tithe to the church in bushels of wheat.* This was also a time where consciousness was evolving from [the big G-Man] being vengeful and full-of-wrath, to being a kind and loving [big G-Man]. *Jesus opened a can of whoop-ass on the money-changers in the Temple, so there was something going on in there regarding money. Maybe Jesus was not so kind and loving after all.*

Stories were the way religions of earlier times made their point. There were lots of religious stories, the most popular and familiar (Old Testament) stories to most would be: Moses and the burning bush and some commandments carved in stone; parting of the Red Sea; Noah and the **Ark of the Covenant** *(oops, got that story mixed up with an Indiana Jones movie).* The newer (New Testament) stories include Jesus: healing the sick; calming the seas; walking on water; multiplying the loaves and fishes; raising the dead, etc. etc. and so on.

Along comes Newton who got bopped on the head by an apple and invents *Apple Computer* – oops – he invents gravity *(people just floated around until then),* and then Physics, and starts science on its way. Fairly recently, along comes Quantum Physics, which is a branch of science, and should contain all of science's other best traits, including predictability. The *Finite* is in full-ahead *(using ship terminology).*

The atom in regular Physics had the electron and the planetary model, in which there is no spiritual mind whatsoever. Now in Quantum Physics, the electron is in a probability cloud, involving both brain (which some call the little or false mind) *and* mind. Yesterday, mind was "out." Today both mind and brain are "in" – at least in Quantum Physics!

The evolution of consciousness, from right-brain-only religion with their stories, to left-brain science with all that implies including predictability, and back to the middle where the entire brain – both hemispheres – is witnessed.

Previously science had, among all its branches: weights, measures, equations, and best-of-all predictability. Previously religion had little that was measurable or predictable ... that's its nature. Now Quantum Physics is here: life is better ... or is it worse ... or is it the same? Consciousness and life go on, regardless!

Things will keep transitioning from the invisible to the visible, and science will keep changing and predicting the visible, both via the *Power of Creation* (aka life), *at least until somebody pushes some button!*

The Law of Attraction

There are many, many sources for books, videos, etc. claiming to be Law of Attraction related. Some claim to have a secret (or *The Secret*, a popular movie available to watch on-line, download, or on DVD from many sources) and why it works for some, doesn't work for others, etc. Some include parts of the Law of Attraction which fit into their program, and flat-out deny other aspects. It has become like any other religion. As with any "truth philosophy," (or any philosophy whatsoever) it does not take long for many to glom on, especially for a price.

Think about all the diet regimens out there. Assuming the diet is not simply an out-and-out scam, the diet has worked for someone, and now they are guaranteeing it will work for you. It has probably worked for many – at least for a while – predicated on how much they believed it. And there are literally tons *(pun intended)* of diets. Maybe what actually works is something other than eating fifteen grapefruits a day. Maybe everyone is unique.

There are similarly many get-rich-quick schemes out there, and once again assuming no scam, they each have worked for at least one person. If getting rich quick works for anyone, it worked for the person hawking it – *the person including their notarized bank statement with their scheme would be one.* Buyer beware, as they say *(comprende ignoranus is the Latin term).*

How they actually made their money was often *not* by doing whatever they are selling. *Beware of programs for how to "Get Rich Quick Selling Magazine Subscriptions."* The authors did not get-rich-quick by what they *said* to do, but by selling the "idea" of getting-rich-quick. Get the difference? What actually works is something *other* than the specific method they are pushing. Magazine subscriptions are not part of Getting Rich Quick.

You may consider a teaching *not* starting off with specific claims to help you lose weight, or make you wealthy. Such a non-specific teaching might be more enlightening than others by not being limited to one area. You may also wish to skip over something titled "Get Rich Quick using the Law of Attraction." Realize just the same, "Wealth" aka "Financial Abundance" and beautiful bodies are an important part of our society and culture, which many people are interested in, hence the proliferation of programs *and TV Infomercials.*

You may have figured out by now there is something in common between dieting and getting rich. Other areas of your life that are – or are not – working would include your: health, relationships, job … in fact, every other conceivable area of your life is covered. The areas in your life that are working you are not thinking about, and the areas that are *not* working get reinforced via your "negative" attention. *It's somebody else's fault anyway.*

There is no "don't want" in the Law of Attraction or the Universe in general. There is only attention *to* something. So if you don't want pizza with anchovies, stop thinking about it, and put your attention instead on some other type of pizza – say pepperoni.

Get to know the rules of this game called life, and not just a method for getting rich, because you still may have poor health and no relationships of a significant kind. To say nothing of being overweight! Forget the person with a great body and good health, but who is continually involved in abusive relationships, one after the other, and whose finances are in the toilet. Start with the Law of Attraction in a general way. Buyer beware of too specific programs. There's always at least one person the program presumably worked for. But also remember, every person is unique as a snowflake … completely unique. That being said, there is one point in common: everyone is working for themselves, but in their own unique way. It may take a lot of what some call "work," but what are the other options?

One of the most popular Law of Attraction series is known as the ***Abraham series***. The book, ***The Law of Attraction***, is a compilation of original channeled material (Q & A sessions) by Esther and Jerry Hicks. It is presented in a simple way to be understandable, as well as offering explanations, examples, and easy exercises. A simple explanation of some aspects of the Law of Attraction is contained within it, which is furthered by other Abraham works.

The very base of the Law of Attraction is more than just a philosophy, since physicists are currently working with it. The expressions "Like attracts like," or "Birds of a feather flock together," are a couple of popular slogans expressing the Law of Attraction in a familiar way.

Merging "Like attracts like" beliefs with energy, gives us good or bad outcomes, predicated on whether our beliefs are good or bad, in our individual opinion. If you believe going to your mailbox will only result in a bad outcome (bills), guess what you get when you go to your mailbox? A bad outcome. Hint: bills. Such a scenario is illustrated in the movie ***The Secret***. One other little secret: you can't rain on anyone else's parade while you're getting yours.

If you really, *really* <u>believe</u> going to your mailbox will result in your receiving unexpected income (with nothing cancelling your belief), guess what's in your mailbox? Unexpected income. There are actual cases like: someone planned a vacation, made reservations and booked tickets, not knowing how they were going to pay for them. They went to their mailbox and received unexpected income in the form of a forgotten insurance settlement in the exact amount they needed. They *desired* the outcome (vacation), *expected* it (booked tickets before ever receiving the income), and *allowed* it to happen.

These terms are used around the Law of Attraction, but explicitly restating them is in order, so here's their definition ("it" is the result):

- desire – a combination of thinking about it, wanting it, and putting your attention on it with a certain level of intensity
- expect – it to happen
- allow – make the decisions that come your way via coincidences, etc. will allow it

According to the Law of Attraction, *desire* is the first step, combining the emotion of wanting and thinking into one step, and the intensity of attention to the outcome is also involved. If there is little attention to the outcome, you really don't desire it and it is not going to happen.

This sets the wheels of the Universe in motion, forming the invisible results which Abraham says are "waiting in escrow." [24] We need only to *expect* and *allow* (be worthy of) the outcome; some cases might involve making decisions with appropriate action to see the invisible become visible. Your thoughts *will* attract similar thoughts, others with the same-type thinking, or co-incidences like unexpected income which will now ultimately form the now visible (or almost visible) result. The results become visible when everything lines up.

The Universe knows only emotion and outcome according to *desire*, and its job is to deliver results accordingly. It does not differentiate between what a person would consider good or bad. Therefore if you're living in fear and order a pizza, a pizza with anchovies is delivered, as you might *expect* when you ordered pepperoni.

---

[24] Hicks, Esther; Hicks, Jerry (2009-09-01). The Vortex: Where the Law of Attraction Assembles All Cooperative Relationships (p. 177). Hay House. Kindle Edition.

A wrong pizza order may be "explained" in rational terms, especially now you have "figured out" that a person with the same last name always orders pizza with anchovies; so anchovies is what you expect ... even when you order pepperoni. Explaining the error adds intensity.

If your life is full of gratitude, you *will* get a pepperoni pizza delivered, now as you may presumably *expect*. You *allowed* the result into your life by paying for a pizza with one extra, which further reinforces your belief. A pizza with anchovies is "bad," while a pepperoni pizza is "good," but only to you. The Universe *(and the pizza place)* doesn't care. Anchovies are "good" to someone, as you have already figured out.

It's a belief behind knowing you will have whatever the subject of your *desire* is, and the *expectation* or faith in the result, that's one important point. Continually stepping on the bathroom scale to *reinforce* losing excess weight which you *knew you could do anyway* is a very different proposition than continually stepping on the scale to see you hadn't lost the weight you knew you couldn't lose *anyway*. It's the belief (knowing) that counts.

One of the important points is the emotion from doing something that feels good. That is our "emotional sense" that lets us know we're on track. In religion they often call the non-physical self the "soul." In one **Simpsons** episode, the next-door-neighbor (mega-Christian) Flanders kids were singing the Christian kiddie song "I got the joy, joy, joy, joy down in my heart ... down in my heart to stay!" Do you have joy in your soul? Does it feel good to lose weight if that is your *desire*?

In the **Seth Material**, Seth says in some realities, time goes backwards from our forward linear time progression. No-one living in our reality could understand how time going backwards would be *(except comedians who talk about ending life with an orgasm)*. The **Seth** and the **Abraham series**, as well as other channeled material, might go a little over the edge for some. Stick it out for a minute.

In ***The Law of Attraction*** book, Abraham is asked what the "Laws of the Universe" are. Abraham explains basic fundamental laws, like gravity, 3-D space, and time are not present in other realities, so Abraham calls them *agreements* instead. [25]

Let's consider starting with the scenario Abraham calls "creating by default" where one is a victim, takes what comes along, and thereby gets results that reinforces their view of reality. Normally Universal Laws do not correspond with our *agreements*.

Abraham explains the only three Laws of the Universe present in *all* realities are (the phrase "The Law" precedes each one to keep them consistent):

1. The Law of Attraction
2. The Law of Deliberate Creation, and
3. The Law of Allowing [26]

You need to *experience* and become comfortable with one to move on to the next (just "understanding" the law is not enough) ... they build on each other.

Try creating on purpose instead of "creating by default" using the Law of Attraction Universal Laws. It may be confusing when the first law is titled the same as the entirety.

Law #1: The Law of Attraction. Everything in your *Finite* reality is comprised of vibrating energy. When you also vibrate at a similar level, you make it possible for what you experience through the other senses (i.e. those situations, experiences, and people vibrating at the same level as you) to be *attracted* to you, hence

---

[25] Hicks, Esther; Jerry Hicks (2007-05-17). The Law of Attraction (pp. 44-45). Hay House, Inc. - A. Kindle Edition.
[26] Hicks, Esther; Jerry Hicks (2007-05-17). The Law of Attraction (p. 24). Hay House, Inc. - A. Kindle Edition.

the name of Law #1 as well as the philosophy. The first Law of Attraction controls going from invisible potential and energy, to the visible comprising your reality. Your programming, filters, and beliefs become what attracts things to you, and your reality is thereby completely formed in this manner by your very own *Power of Creation* (your perception).

Things might become visible as opposed to attracted, but that may just be semantics. If what is attracted becomes visible, what's the difference? The Law of Attraction is reflected in sayings, and variations occur in other "old wives tales" like "you can tell a person by the people he hangs with." The "friends" are one visible indicator. There are so many sayings, and the philosophy is woven into many children's and fairy tales ... there are too many to mention.

Once our brain is wrapped around Law #1, we can start to address deliberately creating our reality via Law #2. One may say, "You cannot sit there and tell me I deliberately created my health problem, can you?" Of course not. Not many would create their own problems, unless their psychological payback was to be on TV!

Psychology gets into paybacks and all the other things psychology gets into, so you may just get on TV as your particular payback. All the other situations, literally, like relationships, jobs, money, *and yada-yada-yada* fall into the same ballpark, and you may get onto **Oprah, Dr. Phil**, or the **Jerry Springer show** if your condition is bad enough. "Who would deliberately do *that* to themselves?" one is tempted to ask. Remember, many people watch with intensity, if not want to be on, these shows. So they *are* deliberately doing it to themselves without knowing it.

Law #2: The Law of Deliberate Creation, builds on the previous law. Remember, you neither create nor destroy energy, but only change its form. So on the journey from potential to reality, one needs to be careful about what your state-of-mind (attitude) is, so you thereby have a "good" mindset and attract a good reality (to see and experience). Such is the first part of deliberately creating your reality ... after all, would you rather have a "good" or "bad" reality?

The first way to deliberately create your reality is to control your state-of-mind, which is easily done when you are aware how it works. Suppose you are now going around much of the time with anger, hatred, and revenge on your mind, or some other "negative" thinking. Some will think they are never able to forgive – this implies a choice. Remember the scenario: taking the poison yourself, while expecting the other person to die? Such is non-forgiving, so "I hope that person's life is working out for them," to paraphrase Dr. Phil. A "negative person" is creating by default, and is probably not pleased with life.

As the negative person continues to experience one bad reality after another, their reality further reinforces their world-view, and they will continue to get pizza with anchovies unless they change vendors, and they are already using the only shop that delivers to their address. So let's change their state-of-mind – it's easy. Imagine, for instance, instead of anger, hatred, and revenge, he or she switches their attitude to joy and gratitude, or other "positive" thinking.

An attitude or feeling of joy *("down in my heart to stay!")* can be accomplished for what a nice day it is, even if it's raining. Some people like rain; just watch the movie where the guy is jumping in the puddles and twirling his umbrella. Look at kids: they don't have any problem with rain. *Some take whatever they're handing out – what choice do you have? Be miserable ... and spread it around? Complain? (Yeah, that works ... especially for everybody else!) Or you can choose to be happy regardless of the weather!*

In terms of gratitude, you can be grateful for nothing more than having a home with an address that gets pizza deliveries. There, you've done it! You've upgraded your mindset to one of joy and gratitude.

Eventually the good thinking will take over, and you can let go of the bad ("nothing but anchovies") thinking, and switch to the type of gratitude outlined above. Eventually there will be nothing but "good" thinking remaining, and you will finally have a pepperoni pizza delivered!

If you were to think about it using words, intelligence, and reason, the pizza shop must have changed order takers, or the other person with the same last name moved. There's always an explanation or excuse for the rational brain. Sooner or later you will get anchovies again if you switch back to creating by default.

Of course, you may easily slip back into your old patterns of anger, hatred, and revenge thinking, but like they teach you in some forms of meditation, when the "monkey mind" chatter comes back, be present with it, and just let it go. So when the "bad" thinking comes back, just tell yourself "Oh, there's *that* again!" and return to joy and gratitude instead. Keeping track of your emotions applies to what you are thinking, not just to what you are doing. *Wash your hands (twice) of anchovies. Employees need to wash their hands, says the sign!*

> *Sign, sign, everywhere a sign*
> *Blocking out the scenery, breaking my mind*
> *Do this, don't do that . . . can't you read the sign?*
> **Five Man Electrical Band**

You may be thinking "that sounds hard," but it really isn't. In the Law of Attraction as taught by Abraham, they suggest monitoring your feelings as this gauge, which will be either good or bad (one or the other, but not both), and thereby create your good or bad reality via your perceptions. Are you feeling good, or are you feeling bad *right now*? Monitoring your feelings doesn't sound all that hard, does it?

Then there is the person with a recurring health problem; OR a "bad" job or boss, finances, marriage or relationship problems, and the list goes on to include every problem situation occurring to you. These are problems that literally keep recurring to you as you create your reality by default while being a victim of your circumstances. So the person keeps going back to his or her doctor, job, bank, marriage counselor *(or eHarmony)* and getting the same results. Point proved through experience.

Have you ever known someone continually experiencing abusive relationships? Even if he or she meets someone that seems nice and well balanced, sooner or later there they go … abused again. Abused people have actually gone out and bought their *abusor* a handgun as a present, *presumably because the abuse they were undergoing wasn't enough until they were pistol-whipped or shot.* So the question recurs: "Why would anyone do *that* to themselves?" And the answer also keeps recurring: "Well, they wouldn't … *deliberately.*"

All the problem scenarios happen when you are *not* deliberately creating your reality. But don't give up just yet! Wherever you are in life, you got there as the end-result of all the decisions you have made. In a good manner, you start to make better decisions, and ultimately turn your life from bad to good. Sooner or later you are at a better position in your life. Don't even try to monitor your thoughts: just the *thought* of monitoring your thoughts is a thought, and that's just too many. There's only good or bad emotions – that's only two.

The *second* way to *deliberately* create your reality: monitor whether you *feel* good or bad (remember, there's only two choices) as you're thinking or doing <whatever>. If it feels **bad**, don't do it – if it feels **good**, do more of it and more like it. This, too, is not all that hard … doing something that feels good is not all that hard, is it? Easier than doing what feels bad, is it not? Be aware of what you are thinking or doing, and whether it makes you feel good or bad … but continually staying aware *is* a discipline.

Coming into this existence, our senses help us navigate our physical environment. They are: sight, sound, smell, taste, and touch. No one teaches us how to use senses, they are learned in our first couple years. Your Mother may teach you a rule to look both ways before crossing, but that's a rule about looking both ways, not how to look. Another rule reinforced by experience is not to touch a hot stove.

No one seems to know why we do some other things. The meaning behind the handshake is well known. It's to demonstrate to the other person, I am *not* holding a weapon. It has evolved into the handshake rule of greeting or trust. There are those that crush the other person's hand, or judge the person as limp and ineffective *(a wet fish)* via the handshake. Everyone has their own handshake and interpretation of others going on. How do you *feel* when giving or receiving a handshake? Good or bad? Intuition helps.

A harder one to "understand" is the smile.

> *If you smile at me, I will understand*
> *'Cause that is something everybody everywhere does*
> *In the same language*
>
> ### *(CSNY);* Wooden Ships

Scientists, doctors, and whomever are still trying to figure out exactly what facial muscles, etc. are used to effect a smile, and what it does – despite the obvious. There are those faking smiles, but everyone has their own smile (or multiple smiles, if one likes to use different ones), and likewise interpret others' smile, even though we're all doing them in the same language. How do you *feel* about giving a smile? What if you are faking it? What if the other person is faking it – use intuition or one of the oracles.

There's this other, for lack of a better word – "sense" – we all have but no one thinks about *at all*. This sense is emotions or feelings, which are either good or bad. Either one or the other, but not both, and not something else. They tell us whether or not we're on track with the intention we set for ourselves before we came into this physical reality, as well as more immediate feedback. For more explanation, refer to the Abraham book *The Law of Attraction*.

Some people won't try dancing unless they can go out on the floor and immediately dance like John Travolta in *Saturday Night Fever* (white suit, pointing fingers, and all), or wouldn't go skiing unless they can do a double-black-diamond trail (not by mistake, and not sliding down the trail on their butt, ski garb and all) the first time out. One may extend this to losing weight. After all, if you are already an expert dancer, skier, and at a perfect weight, why bother? The skinny is *(pun intended)* you need to start from wherever you are.

In much the same way as letting go of "bad" thinking, similarly there is letting go of doing things that make you feel bad. Do it even if doing so only makes you feel a little bit good. Let go of it if it doesn't. Try dancing, skiing, or losing weight … but only if it feels good.

Does it *really* make you feel good to have people come to your sick bed to take care of you, and hear your complaints when you're in constant pain? Does it *really* make you feel good to continually yammer on to your friend over the phone about your abusive significant other? How good does it *really* make you feel buying a carton of cigarettes at the convenience store, especially when the price keeps going up?

What would make you feel good, *really* good, at least for a while? Getting out of your sick bed and sitting in a chair, even if you may feel some pain? Tell those doting on you, you will be needing less of their attention as you get well. It may be just as hard for the person doing the doting (psychologists call it a mutually co-dependent relationship, among many other terms).

There are some professions almost requiring you to smoke to get a break, and go outside in the freezing cold to yammer with your buds. In reality, wouldn't it make you *really* feel better *not* to do that for a day? How about two days? Your buds may miss you, but you will come up with something. How about stopping sucking down those cigarettes? Not even lighting up the first one and drawing smoke deep into your lungs feels so good any more. *Now* do you feel better?

After the "bad" situation is gone, you may look around and say "nothing much has changed!" There is a *Zen* proverb: Before enlightenment, you chop the wood and carry the water. After enlightenment, you chop the wood and carry the water. That's what enlightenment is to some ... being (en)lightened of some previous bad behavior. Everything else is the same.

Most likely, the "bad" behavior will come roaring (or crawling) back, but as in anything bad, stay present with it and keep letting it go. Most New Year's resolutions fail, because as soon as the resolver eats the first doughnut, takes the first drink, or sucks down the first cigarette, there goes *that* resolution. And it takes less, probably much less, than a month. Maybe a day. Another failure is added to the growing list of failures in life. Point proved, once again!

As they say, "If at first you don't succeed, try, try again!" Come back with an even stronger *resolve* to lose those nasty pounds. How about *resolving* to stop smoking those cigarettes that *really* are making you (and everyone around you) sick, as well as helping to keep you broke. Throw away the rest of those doughnuts, and crush the remaining cigarettes, even if it says "crush proof pack." There is not a crush proof pack ever invented that remains "crush proof" after being run over by a car! *I heard a New Year's Resolution whereby you resolve to never make another New Year's Resolution. Now there's one you can definitely keep!*

If it is worth doing for New Year's, it's worth doing on any day. Is it worth stopping smoking only on New Year's? Regardless, after a while, you will look around and realize you really *do* feel better, have lost those pounds, or stopped smoking those cigarettes. If you can resist long enough to get past the craving, soon enough you'll realize you will never be doing *that* again! The *point of power* is driving past the convenience store or donut shop and *not* turning in to buy cigarettes or donuts. You really don't *need* coffee (especially since there's a pot at work!) You are grateful, and feel good! See how easy it is to feel good?

If you hadn't noticed by now, none of this involved "doing" anything like joining weight watchers, or smokers anonymous. There is nothing you need to "do" except acquire the correct mindset. Sometimes, of course, gaining the right state-of-mind is going to require discipline, like getting out of bed and lose a doting friend, or even leave home if that's where you're getting abused. Get into the right mindset, and do only the things that feel good.

If doing something makes you feel good, like learning how to play an instrument, then by all means have at it. Feeling good is the object. Just don't outline specific results, like learning to play a specific instrument *and* getting a new significant other. If you forget about any specific requirements, often something much better will show up from infinity. That wasn't the instrument you wanted to play anyway … singing is better. Hint: When a goal has an "and" or "or" in it, it is really two goals.

For instance, suppose you forget about the "significant other" part of the goal. Maybe you start singing at a local Karaoke bar, and there she is: "The Love of Your Life." She makes you forget all about the unavailable co-worker you've been pining over for years. *Now* you feel good!

Religious Science teaches us not to outline the "house on the corner with the white picket fence," but instead consider qualities like "near to work" and "affordable mortgage payments." A house will show up to match any requirements set by intention, but chances are good it will *not* be the one on the corner with the white picket fence *(which was just a **Money Pit** anyway)*.

The Law of Attraction goes above and beyond this to say "The Universe *will* provide the corner white-picket-fence house," just as long as you don't start fretting over the mortgage, which eliminates it by spiritual law. (Fretting over the mortgage adds the cancelling "but" factor.) Feeling good is the object.

Now that you have embraced "Like attracts like," have changed your state-of-mind, and are feeling good, you're well on the way to embracing Law #3: The Law of Allowing. Remember, Law #3 builds on Law #2 which builds on Law #1.

Law #3 builds on the first two, but you *will* have to take some action as good outcomes appear as per spiritual law. You will need to pick up the phone and order a pepperoni pizza to be delivered, now that you have changed your mind and changed your life. You will need to NOT turn into the convenience store or donut shop. Doing something, or sometimes more correctly *not* doing it, is easier than the opposite. Do what feels good – it's easier. *Really.*

Law #3: The Law of Allowing has two sides. The harder part for people to accept is: while you are allowing what you want into your life (by doing or *not* doing things that occur to you in previous steps), it is important to let everyone else do whatever it is they are doing. Who cares if they're buying cigarettes or ordering anchovy pizza? You thereby allow them to attract *their own* good results into *their own* existence, as you're allowing yours in. Or whatever else they are doing. No judgement about cigarettes or anchovies! And this is the kicker: *even if it would appear what they are doing is trying to disallow what you are doing.*

BTW – I have no more right to control what someone else is doing any more than they have to control me. That's just the way it is, even if the control freaks and politicians say something differently. As far as yourself, you allow into your life only what you choose to allow in.

It always *seems* easier to get someone *else* to do (or not) something instead of doing something yourself … always. A little example is in order, so we'll use something generic. Both sides are adamant about making the other side do, or not do, what they want. One side wants to force you to do something, where the other side says they don't want to. The battle is joined by the sides that *want* to do battle. Does doing battle *seem* easier than just doing <whatever>? For those that want to do battle, it is. *Especially when, if you lose the battle, you need to do it anyway! But now it's their fault and another battle looms.*

This is in keeping with Law #3: The Law of Allowing; you only *get* in your experience what you *allow in.* If you really don't want to do it, and do not *allow* anyone or anything into your experience to make you do it, then you won't have to do it. If you're on the other side of the political spectrum, and want to *make* someone do it, then you *will* find someone to ultimately engage in the resultant political battle. *The battle is all part* of whoever's reality that wants to allow battle in, which would be *both sides* wanting to *fight* over doing, or *not* doing it.

There goes the need for control freak laws coercing someone to do or not do something … it's all up to you. The person trying to force somebody to do (or not) something, still needs a law that says so. But remember, Law #3 says you can't rain on anyone else's parade.

To say nothing of wars fought in the rain. How many wars would have been unnecessary had someone not tried to force someone else to do something? Hint: All of 'em. *(Actually, the spoils-of-war thing is just an excuse for forcing someone.)* So until everyone signs up for creating duality otherwise, we'll still need laws and wars, but you won't get involved if it doesn't *feel* good.

As for all the people hawking a "cure" for something; the world is filled with people offering solutions for a price – such is the way it is. People accept or reject the "solution" predicated on the price and what they think it will do for them, and whether it professes to make them feel better *(ever hear of the placebo effect?)* There was a time preceding Patent Medicine Laws and the FDA, in which everybody was offering a cure for anything (the drugs everyone was pushing had some derivative similar to cocaine). Now there's Big Pharma and TV commercials and pills with colors.

This fellow went to a psychologist for a free consultation. After explaining his problem, the psychologist says: "It appears from your problem, you will need 1 hour of intensive therapy twice-a-week for 3 months, followed by weekly therapy for 3 more months, and a follow-up twice-a-month for 1 and one-half years or more until the problem goes away. My therapy price is $ one hundred dollars per hour." The fellow looks at the Doctor, scratches his chin and replies "Sure, Doc, that solves your problem, but what about mine?"

An internet video shows a solution for why the Law of Attraction only works for a few. The reasons why it did not work for most, was exactly what **The Law of Attraction** book (featured prominently in the video) explains most people are doing wrong. The course author did what the book said would not work, over and over again, and guess what? It didn't work. But the course author knew what to do to fix it for *you* – for a price. If enough people ordered the course, that would solve the course author's problem!

The proposed solution was a course of workbooks and CDs or DVDs, *probably with a money-back guarantee to work in 60-days, which seems to be a standard today.* I'm sure the course was exactly what you would find in **The Law of Attraction** book itself, using different words, but the course is some multiple of price. The long and short: if the workbooks, etc. help, then go for it, but there is no need. If it makes you *feel* good, do it! But there's the same caveat: as long as you are not raining on anyone else's parade (as stated in Law #3: The Law of Allowing).

According to the Law of Attraction, our consciousness will ultimately attract thoughts and events according to our *desires*, and thereby reinforce our thinking as reality. We can *deliberately* have a "positive" mindset, while *allowing* others to do so for themselves.

But don't worry – you can always purchase a course *guaranteed* to produce the life you want. They'll be happy to refund the purchase price after your life is not completely changed after 60 days … such is the nature of marketing. *You can claim your refund, but you probably won't. Speaking of refunds, have you heard the marketing shtick by the tax preparation geeks that guarantees you the biggest refund? How many returns do you have to file? OMG!*

Dis-engaging the Ego aka the rational mind

Two hemispheres of our brain control the different sides of our body. The left-side is the rational hemisphere which controls the right side of our body; the emotional right hemisphere is linked to infinity and controls the left side of our body. In other words, if you are right-handed the rational hemisphere of your brain is on the left. It is the opposite for left-handed people.

The rational side of the brain houses the intellect which operates via logic, reasoning, and words. The left-brain assigns words to everything, which automatically limits any references it might make to infinity by only alluding to it. The rational side of the brain also contains the ego, whose job it is to protect us. In the **Don Juan series**, it is often said the ego goes overboard in its job, and so turns from a guardian into a jealous guard.

Without the ego, you cannot plan *how* money will come in, or any other "goal" you may have, for planning invokes the ego which knows only how you did it before, and how to protect you. There were many times when money was needed, and it showed up in a totally unplanned manner – therefore my ego (reason) could *not* have been involved.

The rational, intellectual, or ego side of the brain has words, thinks in words, and is limited to our reality. It performs according to intentions you have set, which is fine, but it does not perform "word-less" miracles you cannot explain. The emotional side of the brain has NO words, and *can* perform "miracles" (as they are often called.) Try explaining serendipity using words. The best you can do is allude to it. *OMG! I can't believe who just called me!*

On literally the other hand, is the emotional side of our brain, linked to infinity. It is supposed to be on the right side of our brain, once again for right-handed people. Left-handed people have their rational side of the brain on their right *(or starboard for those nautically inclined)* and the emotional side on their left. *To make a short story long, lefties are the opposite of righties. If you are ambidextrous, which side-of-the-brain is which is unknown.*

Never the right and left shall meet. Well, almost never. *"Never say never" as they say. They also say "Never say always!" Every rule has an exception, which probably accounts for many other sayings.* There are some creative activities which use words to express themselves, like writing and music. Truly creative activities come from the *Infinite* side, whereby words come from the *Finite*. So the two sides *do* meet on occasion … or at least cooperate.

What's the commonality between knowing or *not* knowing about spiritual matters and receiving the literal payback? It would appear forgetting about it is a key. In fact, the last step in what Religious Science calls a treatment (affirmative prayer) is the release step, which involves forgetting about it. So don't continually dig up the plant to see if it's growing. The process starts with the spiritual work; *then, like they say in Jersey: (spelled phonetically) Fug-ged'da-bou-dit (forget-about-it).*

Transcendental Meditation (TM) claims, as an objective, to equalize the disparate frequencies of the two sides of the brain. Metaphysically such a result might be considered good. TM would heartily claim equalizing the frequencies of the two sides of the brain is a good thing.

When you try to "think" of a solution to anything, or explain your idea to anyone else, you are using words and have thereby engaged the left side of the brain, housing the ego which only knows past history and how to protect you. The best the ego can do is re-shuffle history to present a solution; the worst the ego can do is to tell you that you cannot do it. The way the ego is defined here is *not* creative with brand-new, never-before-tried, out-of-the-box ideas.

So, if you are looking for a brand-new solution, by definition you must be creative and cannot explain yourself or your ideas to anyone without using words and engaging the ego. At some point you may need words and numbers, possibly in the form of a business plan, to explain your idea, but not at first. Remember, Edison did not re-hash old ideas to invent the light bulb. If his ego was in charge, he either would have:

- not had anything to do (the ego could not supply previous *successful* accomplishments regarding the light bulb ... from anyone, anywhere)
- not had to do anything (the ego readily supplies what Edison had already *successfully* done, which does *not* include the light bulb)

In either case, not having anything to do is good, right? Edison wouldn't agree. So relying on the ego gives him nothing to do; instead, he tapped into possibility and created the incandescent light bulb. He probably felt good, too! He did not consider the 9,999 "failures" as such (according to him, he invented the light bulb on the 10,000th try) when he was asked about them.

Having looked at Edison, his other patentable inventions like the wax recording device that eventually turned into vinyl records, nor the movie camera, are examined. Looking at other creators, we can consider whether they used their reason exclusively. Hint: they didn't, especially if they "invented" something brand new.

We'll look at just one other creator mentioned elsewhere in another context. He was not previously mentioned by name, but his "invention" was ... the phone by Alexander Graham Bell, which ultimately became today's smart-phone. He built on others' past accomplishments; if Bell were just have read technical journals, he then added creativity. The ego can't do both! *Was Bell's mother known as "Ma Bell?"*

If Bell tapped into the *Infinite*, he would need a right-brain link. The telegraph was already around sending electrical impulses down a wire. So he both tapped existing creation and applied creativity to refine the electrical impulses, using both sides of his brain. We don't know how many journals he read using words and his left-brain, but he added creativity, which can only come from the right-brain via its link to all those possibilities. *Can you hear me now?*

What *is* important: creativity taps into the *Infinite* for possibilities, which others added to in the past. If you just want to just re-hash old ideas, then have-at-it, but your name probably won't become a household name. If you want to be the most creative you can be, you will have to allocate some CPU brain-time to the side of your brain that contains a link to the *Infinite*.

So, if you want to engage creativity, you must first put your attention on your idea, then allow creativity to chime in. BTW, allowing creativity in neither engages your reason or your ego. Can you tell me using words what part of reason is involved in allowing communications from the *Infinite* in? Hint: don't try too hard!

Imagination vs. Visualization

There is an invisible part of our Universe (the *Infinite*) comprised of possibilities and energy, not considering other invisible parts. It is linked to the half of the brain which operates without words, which is also known as our right-brain emotional side. Some would say it is an older part of the brain, if one is operating in forward-going linear time. Hint: in our *Finite* reality, we all operate in the same time-frame.

Current studies show some animals, like doGs, undeniably exhibit emotions as evidenced by some of their features. We know what the emotion of grief is, but show me a doG that has lost his best friend, but remains too grief stricken (and not extremely "happy") about going out for a walk or eating their dinner, as they provide a good example of living in-the-moment.

Animal behaviorists say look for additional body language in doGs other than "smiling" or wagging their tail. Dogs seem to know some words, but such is very limited. My doGs know "out" and "hungry," even if it's only a matter of training like "give me your paw" or "roll over." Words are the equivalent of left-brain activity in humans.

Even animals with the most advanced vocabulary, as in the African Grey Parrot, have only a relatively limited vocabulary compared to most humans. They are also limited in their word-defined reasoning ability, even if they possess some psychic skills we have yet to learn more about in ourselves. It would seem they have no emotions alluded to by any of their words, if indeed they have anything resembling emotions at all. Maybe their emotions pass too quickly.

Pathwork, a channeled philosophy espousing emotional "maturity" and training, says emotions are supposed to be intense, yet brief. Minimizing emotions in Western Culture happens for most men and some women, *but that's Western Culture for you! Everyone knows real men don't cry, but some women seem to go for men that do. Men are allowed to be angry at sports.*

People have words to *describe* emotions, but the words only *allude* to the emotion, since emotions have no words. Take the emotion of "fear" for instance. Try to describe it further with words, and about the farthest you may get would be "a gut-wrenching feeling." Additionally, the same words might also describe other emotions. Men may get a gut-wrenching feeling from anger after their sports team loses.

"Fear" is a *feeling*, and we also know the difference between it and other emotions like "joy" and "gratitude," but trying to explain them with words would be like trying to describe a color, or what something tastes like. This is one reason why emotions operate without words, and people tend to say the part of the brain controlling emotions is older. Some say the sub-conscious is located in an older part of the brain because words are a relatively recent addition in the evolution of consciousness.

Literally on the other side of your head is the hemisphere of the brain known as the rational side, which deals with intelligence, logic, and reasoning. It houses the ego, which supposedly protects us, but often acts as a jealous guardian of our safety, which says much about its overshot purpose. The left side of the brain operates exclusively *with* words and reason, including math and equations, *which is especially useful for mathematicians and scientists!*

Remember, the ego is supposed to protect us from harm, but often overdoes itself and protects us from anything and everything. There are those saying all events from our life are remembered, even if not consciously so, and the memories have been subsequently relegated to our sub-conscious via programming. Some claim the memories are still there and in operation for the ego's use – memories thought long gone are still there controlling behavior.

Now that we've had a little review discussion of the right- and left-brain (the *Infinite* and the *Finite*), let's consider visualization verses imagination. Hint: the differences are mostly semantic except as discussed below.

Many philosophies promote visualization … not just spiritually related philosophies. There has been research scientifically or statistically demonstrating when you visualize making a sports shot (tennis, golf, or basketball, etc.), you improve the player's ability to make that shot when it becomes available, as well as literally improving the player's strength if appropriate. Sports examples abound, as well as for other disciplines like test taking.

There is not a problem with this method *per se*, but it falls short on one account. Basically this form of visualization engages the ego, which turns on the memory of what the person has previously done or learned. And there is the key: what he or she has previously done or learned.

So the ego steps in to protect you, and the visualization exercise has your ego providing numerous examples from what you had previously successfully done, or learned about how others did it. No problem, except visualization comes from your previous accomplishments, or an experience *by someone else*. The sports figure has probably made the shot before – many times – or at least watched films of someone else making the shot. What if you're trying something brand new, or want to "think outside the box?"

That's where imagination as opposed to visualization comes in. Serena Dyer, like her father Wayne, likes to quote people as in Einstein when he said:

> *"Imagination is everything. It is the preview of life's coming attractions. Imagination is more important than knowledge."* [27]

So Wayne Dyer in Serena's book, predictably follows with another quote by Einstein, who says

> *"Logic will take you from A to Z. Imagination will get you everywhere."* [28]

The *Infinite* provides synchronicity. This is one difference between visualizing vs imagination … *Finite* vs *Infinite.*

You *imagine* your new company or idea where money is no object. You may *visualize* making out a business plan, taking it to a bank, then taking out a loan using your house as collateral. Maybe you visualize getting relatives interested in your idea who then become known as the "Angel Investors" written about in entrepreneurial magazines. The ego gets its knowledge from magazines, college classes, or night-school using A to Z logic.

If you want to do something brand new that neither you nor anyone else has ever done before, you will have to use the link to infinite intelligence – you will have to use imagination instead of visualization. Imagine yourself as successful with the money pouring in, even though you have never done anything with this new idea before. Nor has anyone else.

---

[27] Dyer, Serena J.; Dyer, Wayne W. (2014-06-16). Don't Die with Your Music Still in You: My Experience Growing Up with Spiritual Parents (p. 87). Hay House, Inc.. Kindle Edition.
[28] Dyer, Serena J.; Dyer, Wayne W. (2014-06-16). Don't Die with Your Music Still in You: My Experience Growing Up with Spiritual Parents (p. 140). Hay House, Inc.. Kindle Edition.

When you imagine, you are communicating directly with the *Infinite*. When you meditate, you are opening a channel to be used by the *Infinite* to communicate back via ideas, synchronicity, *et al.* Pay attention to intuition, for it contains additional ways communication returns from the *Infinite*.

The proof is where?

I play the harp at a master musician level. So you want to hear? You'll have to take my word for it. There's also the cow-bell. *You can hear me play that.*

These are close to the hardest and the easiest Western instruments to play. The point is, the proof is in the demonstration. Someone once said "The proof is in the pudding" *whatever that means. Anyone have any pudding with proof in it?*

Regarding Ben Franklin and kites, electricity was around before kites. If a law of electricity never does anything, what would be the point? At least there was lightning. Now there's computers, smart-phones, and tall buildings. If laws or principles about *anything* never actually <u>do</u> anything, what would be *that* point? *Assuming a law of "sound," it gets drowned-out by the sound of one hand clapping. RIGHT or WRONG?*

By now, you might have determined a pattern. If you have equations and predictions surrounding it, it is "proven" by science, right? Even if scientists have *not* given us an equation and predictions about it, the fact you can see <whatever-it-is> at work is proof enough. Is there an equation and predictions about playing a harp or cow bell? But even if you have explicit measurements and instructions regarding how to cook the roast, some people are just bad cooks. *Maybe they just don't have "brown-thumbs" (a take-off on green-thumbs and gardening) although that is disturbingly disgusting.*

No further knowledge about electricity is needed to turn on a light. *What color thumb would you need then?* Presumably *(hopefully)* someone knew more than you about electricity when they put in a light switch connected to a light bulb. *Ben Franklin or Thomas Edison may have.*

Reality and life are referred to as the *Finite* and the *Power of Creation* respectively, and the *Power of Creation* is additionally synonymous with perception. The *Infinite* is invisible, and the *Finite* can change as per the Law of Attraction. But relatively speaking, any changes to the *Finite* are minor. So where's all this other stuff that's supposed to be in infinity?

In the example of Paris on some other map, we know it exists, but never go there. *It's one of those double whammy things. Or maybe it's a double-edged sword. Or maybe it's double trouble. It's double something.*

Pilots have observed UFOs making 90-degree turns at high speed … far outside our "laws" of physics. It is speculated these pilots are witnessing objects that have slightly crossed into our "dimension" but are still operating by their own rules. Within the *Infinite*, actors elsewhere probably have their own rules. *Ever hear of "Area 51?"* Our *Finite* reality functions using linear time. Whether they have linear time (and in which direction it proceeds) is only an object for useless speculation.

Pilots are witnessing other aspects of the *Infinite*, with *Finite* results from other participants using their very own *Power of Creation* we will never "understand." They are close enough to us, *but who would want to eat their pudding?*

> *How can you have any pudding if you don't eat yer meat?*
> ### Another Brick in the Wall; Pink Floyd

So where's the rest of everything? Well, infinity is rather large. In **The Seth Material**, Seth was close enough to our incarnated reality to be channeled. But there was another entity they called Seth II that occasionally came through Seth, and was as far away from Seth (in some other reality) as Seth was to Jane. *Infinity is* *big.* We should be grateful to usually only see our own reality from our dimension.

Dimension is also a word they used in musical-group names:

> *This is the dawning of the Age of Aquarius ... Age of*
> *Aquarius.*

The Fifth Dimension

And they only had five dimensions, not an infinite number.

Concerning "where's the rest?" ... first an analogy. For the *Infinite*, we'll use a yardstick, and for the *Finite* the straight-edge of a plastic protractor or some other six-inch ruler to provide the analogy. One difference would be, in 2D infinity the yardstick would keep going forever, and not stop at thirty-six inches, but we're having an analogy. In the analogy, it is easy for the calculating left-brain to figure out what ratio our smaller ruler is to thirty-six inches, and what percentage our reality is to the *Infinite. It's the kind of thing science would like to know. Not so easy when the base is infinity nor do you know what size your piece of your reality is.*

We'll start by laying the smaller ruler on or next to the yardstick. Of course, the *Power of Creation* (your perception) comes along for the ride and forms the physical from the non-physical. So "why don't we just move our little ruler (our reality) to another place on the yardstick?"

Really? A whole 'nother reality where the rules are probably all different and the characters resemble something from **Star Trek**, dinosaurs, or some TV commercial ... if you can see them at all? It's hard enough to view a little aspect of some dimension that is adjacent to ours, or even nudge ourselves in a good direction inside our own reality. *But you can probably find enough to occupy you for your whole life in Roswell, NM.*

One should wait for being without a body before you sign-up for another reality. *They use sign-up sheets? Inquiring egos want to know.*

How many more six-inch rulers would be needed to fill up the yardstick? That would be five, or five more realities. But taking our analogy back whereby the yardstick becomes truly infinite and goes on forever *(like a geometric line)*, it would take not six, not ten, but an infinite number of ruler-realities. *And the yardstick-line is still 2D if you know geometry!* So is our little ruler-reality, but let's make them *both* infinite, by adding not just Y and Z coordinates, but an infinite number! Remember … infinity is really big.

Mass consciousness falls into, by our definition, the *Infinite* (it's neither visible nor physical) no matter how many categories the left-brain wants to assign. Personal consciousness has been attached to the brain (both visible and physical), placing it into the *Finite*, which makes sense since they are on opposite ends of the consciousness line. The *Power of Creation* places perception and consciousness in charge of creating reality (i.e. infinite realities). *How many consciousness's are in infinity? Inquiring scientific brains want to know. Hint: Lots!*

It seems the *Infinite* has now drawn back into itself the *Finite* and the *Power of Creation* which are now infinite themselves, thanks to the infinite realities they create. Remember … infinity is really, *really* big.

You CAN Get There from Here

Does anyone remember the old joke where some guy was close to his destination, but drove around for hours, apparently lost, before he stopped to ask for directions? After he stopped, he asked an old guy sitting in his rocking chair on his porch how to get there. The old guy continued rocking while looking thoughtful.

Frustrated, the driver asked "So old-timer, have you figured it out?" "Yep" said the old guy in the rocking chair as he spat a vile stream of chawrin' baccy out through his stained teeth onto the ground with a hiss. "You can't get there from here!" *You know it's a joke because no guy would ever stop to ask for directions.*

What we've been looking for forever is something to understand, and thereby consciously use, to best transition our ideas from invisible to visible stuff – from non-physical to physical. Science and cookbooks have provided equations how to manipulate it once it becomes physical. *Preheat your left-brain to three-fifty.*

The "zero state" (as some term it) occurs when there is only the *Infinite*, as we fast forward to the arrival of the *Finite* and the *Power of Creation*. This happens an instant before the *big bang*, where everything is still exceedingly simple, yet capable of embracing complexity. The only things in existence are the three afore-mentioned components: the *Infinite*, the *Finite*, and the *Power of Creation*. Then there is this *big bang*. And complexity. *Besides, of course, people sitting around watching **The Big Bang Theory** on TV.*

Was there also a bunch of people sitting around writing up what is effectively a cosmic religious code to tell everyone how to do everything? Who taught them how to write (right-handed) anyway? Except, of course, lawyers, priests, and other black-robed individuals who have been judging everything since before anything. Nuns have always been around beating people into right-handedness.

There is a dichotomy, or maybe it's a paradox, one encounters trying to make the *Power of Creation* apply the rules of the *Finite* to the *Infinite*, which uses different rules. When there are only three components to everything, ultimately everything must be related to these components, directly or indirectly ... that's *everything*. Anyone is challenged to come up with *anything* not directly or indirectly related to acquiring or manipulating stuff.

Somebody needs to tell scientists that for all their equations, measurements and predictions, they are mostly only working on the *Finite* side – via equations, rules, and predictions, as well as logic and reasoning. They are doing a great job defining the *Finite*, and they won't be running out of equations and rules to work on soon ... they call them theories.

Everyone has forever been trying to explain the *Power of Creation* as well as life itself ... moving things from invisible to visible, then manipulating it. Everything resembling religion or religious philosophy comes from the same point: it doesn't matter if it's *Eastern* or *Western*, more or less *organized* (or even cult-like), *older* or *newer* or *New Age* or *New Thought* – any of them. Some have their own towns in which they serve Kool Aid, others have a dress code that includes Keds.

Since religion has been at it the longest, we'll go to Western Religion first. Religion pre-dated government and laws, so they carved some commandments into stone to keep the rabble in line. The one about not coveting your neighbor's wife really means his stuff, and there was one to the effect of "Thy Shalt Not Steal." *You knew it was scriptural i.e. religious law by "thy" and "shalt." Otherwise it would have read "You shouldn't steal." If it was to be understood by NASCAR viewers, they would have used "Y'all."*

Get your own stuff – which you ultimately do regardless. Make your very own *Power of Creation* (your perception) bring you the stuff you want, from the invisible world of possibilities, to your very own reality via your consciousness.

Let's take a look at some of the wisdom religion has given us via scripture. First, what you see is not based on what you see – what is visible does not come from what is visible. *Say what?* This implies a *transition* from the invisible to the visible. *Or is it infers?* The *Power of Creation* adds: and back again.

Also stated is how a belief is a thought that is thought so often, it needs to be explicitly thought no longer. In scripture it says something to the effect you get what you believe. What you see is based on your beliefs, which in turn are comprised of your programming and filters.

These experiences produce further experiences that reinforce the belief, as explained via **Zen Driving**. This is more of a "double whammy" than a "double-edged sword," since the sword infers *(or implies)* an unforeseen consequence. Since beliefs attract circumstances that further reinforce themselves, they may take a while to re-program (predicated on your beliefs).

Let's look at only the *Infinite*. It does not operate by the same rules as the *Finite* regarding understanding, and has no idea of time whatsoever. The *Infinite* has serendipity, coincidences, and intuition … and who can predict when *they* will happen?

First, you have an inspiration to do something. So you do it, and the *Infinite* has your back. It provides the people, places, and things … almost as if by magic. "Miracle" is a term some use. "Wow," you think, "That was easy. I can do that again." So you do.

The next time you are inspired (in spirit) to do something, the ego takes over a couple steps. You use words, contracts, and goals (things the ego identifies with) to make some steps, which now seem hard. These steps are not as easy as the previous inspiration. It is unclear when or whether the project is finished anyway. Maybe you'll try again … maybe not.

At one point you *do* try again, but with a difference. The third time you have an inspiration, the ego takes over completely. It has all its explanations and excuses lined up to protect you … you are too old / young, too fat / skinny, or too tall / short. My personal favorite is: "I'm too broke to do that," and if you are spiritually in-tune, you will quickly add "right now." If the project is ever started, it is very hard, and most likely remains incomplete.

But don't worry, the *Infinite* always gives you another chance. It might be the exact same thing, or at least the parts you couldn't handle will be similar enough. You have chosen to opt out of pure inspiration via "Free Won't." But it's not that easy to get out of … it will come back to give you another go-at-it. Maybe in another lifetime. Remember, time is of no consequence.

So what animates the *Infinite* that plays by a different set of rules? Animating, here, would be getting the *Infinite* to respond in a timely manner when it doesn't use time. Try imagination. When you imagine yourself successful in a new endeavor, the *Infinite* will respond with synchronicities *et al*. But they take time in our world, and the *Infinite* could-care-less about time. Time is only in our *Finite* reality. So let's try another approach.

There are some relatively new developments in science bringing science and religion closer together. They are: Quantum Physics and the Law of Attraction. The first, as implied by "Physics" in the name, is more science, the latter more religion, but both are now under study by physicists. In a nutshell, you get what you expect. Bad day – bad stuff. Good day – good stuff. Are you having a good life? Remember, Quantum Physics tells us the atom, the building block of nature itself, is intimately related to who is observing it. The Law of Attraction tells us we attract our results.

When born, we are supplied with our senses (sight, sound, smell, taste, and touch) through which we learn to navigate our physical reality. Some rules get added like "Look both ways before crossing," but no-one teaches us how to look. Everyone also has, for lack of a better term, "senses," which everyone experiences but no one knows what they are, where they came from, or what they are for (even though some will say they do). In that sense *(groan)* they are like a smile or sleep.

This is the "sense" of our emotions, and in that sense *(pun intended)* emotions are like a smile. Everybody *(well, most anyway)* smiles and has emotions, and we right-brain "understand" what they mean; all the while scientists are still trying to figure out the smile. What muscles are involved, etc. *and do doGs do it too. When doGs are asleep, that would probably be a good time to let them lie.* Scientists have not even started to address emotions. How would you apply words, logic, and reasoning to that which has none?

Emotions communicate between the physical us, and the non-physical aspect of our being (between the *Finite* and the *Infinite*). They are classified as either "good" or "bad." Go ahead, pick an emotion, any one, and see if it is good or bad for you. Use them.

So the long and short is, you are either having a good or bad: day, life, stuff, or anything and everything in-between. And you *will* attract by the Law of Attraction (or see in nature), the good or bad accordingly. So our answer finally arrives: emotions can be used in a fairly time-specific manner, and produce results in our own linear time.

So this *Infinite* presence produces our separate and individual *Finite* reality, which involves our evolving consciousness via the *Power of Creation*. Can you make your consciousness aka perceptions produce what you want *now*?

Afterword

When I first undertook to study spirituality, later focusing upon how life is *formed* via spirituality, a simple solution was sought. Not one that took seventy-thousand pages to define, as in a spiritual tax-code, interpreted by circular-definition tax lawyers who function in their off-season as priests. Creation does, and always has, occurred *without* words – in silence. *In a linear time-frame, it went on long before the process was written down.*

A spiritual work known as the ***Bible*** exists (as well as many, many other spiritual and religious tomes) that come complete with translations, interpretations, caveats, special dispensations, and ultimately "mysteries" (thanks to George Carlin for that!) There is no single answer everyone can come to agreement on – just like a long tax-form. There are "experts" who spend their whole lives studying a relevant document, and even then they can't agree. There are mysteries. *You know the saying, "There are only two guaranteed things in life: death and taxes." Then there's spirituality and mysteries.*

One of the reasons I was looking for a simple solution, at the beginning of the Universe, who was there to draw up all the rules for everyone else to follow? *Maybe lawyers-from-Hell have always been around!* At one point, the simplest rule-book possible was found, although it still had some complexity to it. Then something *even better* came along, and its complexity was boiled-down to the bare bones *(as in spiritual soup – just add extra-wide noodles).* It keeps getting simpler, as expected.

Different people's suggestions about how to run your life can be followed *risk-free!* You will be guaranteed *(60-day money-back)* to have a productive, satisfying life if you follow their advice. People seem to like following other people's advice. *If your life is not completely satisfying in 60 days, you can get your money back. How many requests will they get from people for a refund?*

The long-and-short is, everyone is unique as snowflakes are supposed to be. *But snowflakes melt too fast to see if this assertion is true. Maybe leaves will work better – they last longer. Maybe grains-of-sand – they last even longer.* Such a study could be #26 on my goal bucket-list, knocking one of the previous 25 off. Another study would have to leave the room in life's game of musical bucket chairs. *Is there a money-back guarantee for the one that left-the-room?*

You are charged with finding your own unique way-in-life. Nobody can tell you how to do it *but if you ate 15 grapefruits a day, you would probably not only lose weight, but be money-back-guaranteed to be sick of grapefruit after wasting away to nothing.*

If you think you have found something that works, go for it. But, as they say, "Buyer beware!" If you continue buying programs that never work, beware! *(comprende ignoranus) BTW, the second word comes from an annual competition where the change of just one letter gives a whole new meaning to a word – in this case the change means "not just stupid, but an a-hole too!"*

What might be considered suggestions have been made generic. There is some mental discipline you will have to undergo if you are to try them, but that's about the only thing you will have "to do." Before you start, be aware that discipline of any kind is not easy. *But at least you won't even have to make a New Year's Resolution to get up early to go to the Gym!*

For the longest time, someone who could tell me "how to do life" was searched for (in vain) putting me firmly into the "vast **majority**." But now I AM joining the "vast **minority**" creating my own visible reality by choice.

Now you have finished reading this, you too are qualified to escape from the "vast **majority**," upgrade your beliefs, and join the "vast *minority*." You now have some tools, as well as additional reading for enhancing and taking control of your life:

- Claim **complete responsibility** for your *entire* life; stop thinking any part of it is a result of something else – by *not* claiming total personal responsibility you become a victim
- Change your programming and filters (your reality) by meditation, applying suggestions or affirmations while in a receptive state
- Stay in a positive mindset (i.e. gratitude, joy) as much as possible to increase your overall level of vibration, and thereby change your reality
- Place your attention on thinking and taking actions that make you *feel* good
- Stay alert for guidance from intuition and related ... meditation opens a channel
- *Desire* what you want out of life specifically, and *expect* it to happen
- Learn to differentiate between left-brain supplied reason, and right-brain intuition
- Make the seeming *coincidental* and *synchronistic* choices coming your way, and do not allow left-brain reason to over-rule your choices
- *Allow* your good outcomes – as well as everyone else's

This is all you have "to do." This is how the Universe works. Only DO that which makes you happy, *unless you like being unhappy; in that case, you could look for a therapist with a money-back guarantee!*

Maintain a positive state-of-mind throughout, adopting positive attitudes as much as possible. You remember the rhyme: "Attitude of Gratitude?"

You need not "make it happen" or keep up with any Joneses. They will be trying to keep up with you. The Joneses will be on *Oprah* after they have literally given up. Or ... you can be on *The Dr. Phil* or *Jerry Springer Show* if you're still grinding your teeth, while holding your breath and turning blue-in-the-face trying to "make it happen." It's up to you.

What do you see when you open your eyes? Reality. Your reality. It can't be anyone else's.

Suggestions for reading and watching

If all you have "to do" is meditate, affirm, and make choices, it seems a lot of time will be left over for other stuff – like reading! Listed here, in roughly the reverse order of importance (most important first) are additional suggestions for reading, listening, viewing *(and doing!)* to reinforce your learning. Some of the suggestions are more recent publications – some older ones have been read over-and-over. Additionally, look at footnoted material.

- Any and all Law of Attraction *"Abraham series"* channeled through Ester Hicks.
    - o You can get DVDs of actual sessions from their website, or through Netflix
    - o The book *The Law of Attraction* by Ester and Jerry Hicks gives a good summary of a lot of their earlier sessions: what the law is and how it operates
    - o *Ask and It Is Given*: Learning to Manifest Your Desires
    - o They have a website: www.Abraham-Hicks.com with lots of good stuff
    - o *Co-creating at its best* has an interview between Wayne Dyer, Abraham, and Esther Hicks
- Dr. Wayne W. Dyer
    - o Author *et al* of works in many media, including PBS specials
    - o *The Shift* – both a movie and a book
    - o *Change Your Thoughts, Change Your Life*: Living the Wisdom of the Tao
- Bob Proctor (as featured in *The Secret*)
    - o A well-renowned prosperity coach, and author of several "self-help" books
    - o *The ABCs of Success*

- Intuition learning from Sonia Choquette, Phd.
  - o Sonia is a well renowned teacher and healer with many books
  - o *Tune In: Let Your Intuition Guide You* to Fulfillment and Flow
- Thomas Troward – writer and lecturer on "intelligence" and mentor to Earnest Holmes, founder of Religious Science
  - o *Bible Mystery and Bible Meaning*
  - o *The Edinburgh and Dore Lectures* on Mental Science
- The *Seth Material* channeled through Jane Roberts
  - o The series contains many books
  - o My personal favorite (and the first book on Spirituality ever to "jump off the shelf" at me) is #3: *The Nature of Personal Reality*
- Napoleon Hill
  - o *Think and Grow Rich*
  - o Many people are familiar with this classic work – longer and shorter versions are available (you don't need the longer one)

This list had to be cut off somewhere, to give you time to tie flies or brew beer, lest you otherwise need to wrap your head in duct-tape so as to contain the messiness when your head explodes.

Many books were read earlier in "dead tree" versions, and have re-acquired some on Kindle. Some seemed simple, or made little sense at the time. Even children's books are often profound.

Glossary

Here you will find definitions for some terms you may not be familiar with, or are used in what might be considered a "non-traditional" manner.

affirmation – a declaration that something is true; used in a first-person, present tense manner, without a cancelling thought; the affirmation uses words from the *Finite* to invoke the *Infinite*; see prayer

Akashic Records – refers to a term started in the late 1800s by Theosophists, and comes from the Sanskrit word for "sky," or "ether." They are a collection of thoughts, events, and emotions from the astral plane representing everything non-physical. There is no scientific evidence for them, nor will there ever be.

atom – known in this writing, as in much of Physics, as "the building block of nature."
   Planetary model – see electron

bad – not acceptable; applied to thinking, beliefs, emotions, or outcomes; obtained by placing your attention with a given the intensity on something; see good

belief – A belief is a thought that is thought so many times it eventually becomes a conscious thought no more, and is pushed down into the sub-conscious where it operates without further attention. If strong enough, it becomes a "knowing."

brain – the organ in the body that is the interface to all the other functions of the body, as well as housing all our memories, programming, and links us to the *Infinite*. What is usually referred to is the most recent addition to other more primitive brain structures, with the most recent being the cerebral cortex or "outer" layer.

left- this side of our brain controls the right side of our body. It is finite, also houses our reasoning facility and ego, and "thinks" in words.

right- this side of our brain controls the left side of our body, and our emotions. It is thought to be involved with our creativity. It is also our link to the *Infinite*. It "thinks" via emotions with no words whatsoever.

wave frequency – using technology measures brain wave frequency from ever smaller and more differentiated areas of the brain.

channel(ed) – Channeled material (wisdom) comes from a non-physical entity (or entities) through a person, operating in a trance-like state, known as a channel. Because of the non-physical nature of the entity, it comes from infinity.

conscious(ness) – operates at many different levels, often below the level of our awareness, and is ultimately responsible for our experiences. We have been programmed in terms of allowing things through our filters, which thereby determine our reality.

mass – those levels of consciousness operating "above" our reality, that provides what are often known as "Laws"

default – the state in which you take no action (aka doing nothing)

duality – that which defines our reality in the sense of not having up without down, right without left, cold without hot, etc.

ego – Psychologists have sometimes defined our ego differently than here; it is part of our reasoning facility, charged with the responsibility of protecting us (from anything and everything known or unknown).

electron – a negatively charged "sub-atomic" particle comprising the atom, along with neutrons (no charge) and protons (positively charged.)

Planetary model – an earlier model of the atom which had all the electrons orbiting the nucleus with specific locations or "vectors"

Probability cloud – the "Quantum Physics" model of the
   atom with electrons around the nucleus in a cloud;
   their location is dependent on the observer
emotion – comes from the right-brain which is linked to the
   Infinite. Emotions are either "good" or "bad" but not both
energy – everything is comprised of energy vibrating at different
   frequencies. Energy cannot be created nor destroyed.
   Thought is energy, and matter is simply energy vibrating at a
   different frequency – it has "changed its form" … the related
   thought is experienced.
evolution – the forward progress of something over time which
   yields a presumably more sophisticated version
faith – a belief in things as yet unseen. This means things have
   taken on a still invisible form, waiting for other factors to
   come into alignment to become visible.
Finite – results are visible and can be physically counted, even if
   large in number (like grains of sand); this term is applied to
   results produced by our brain; see *Infinite*
God – an oft-used (some would say abused) term in religion,
   referred to as [the big G-Man]. This term might be said to
   apply to "Infinite Mind" or infinity.
good –acceptable thinking, beliefs, emotions, or outcomes; see bad
idea – an invisible bit of knowledge (a possibility) that resides in
   the *Infinite*
imagination – creative use of the *Infinite* which encompasses all
   possibilities; see visualize
Infinite – a realm where all possibilities reside. It exists in, and is
   supported by, mathematics where the product of Infinity
   and zero equals one (Unity). "The Infinite" often refers to
   "Cosmic Mind" or [the big G-Man]; see *Finite*
invent(ion) – a term that is used to signify the bringing of an
   idea from the *Infinite* into *Finite* reality, often with legal
   ramifications

intuition – a right-brain function that is often equated with
   spiritual guidance and creativity (along with coincidences,
   serendipity, etc.)

know – an "extra strong" belief that is so strong, you not only
   believe it to be so, but "know" it

logical – see rational

mass – see consciousness

measure – the act of determining how many units (of measure) are
   in something physical which yields a measurement, which
   can then be reproduced

meditate – the process of "going within" (via several methods)
   to slow down your brain to make it more receptive to
   communications from the infinite, or to re-program it

mind – often known as intelligence; when infinite, it is often
   known as "Universal" or "Cosmic;" when finite, it is often
   thought of as contained within the brain

New Thought – one of the more "recent" religious branches of
   Organized Religion, that states what is ultimately realized in
   reality is first thought in mind

objective – a term used both in logic and in Religious Science
   (which refers to the right-brain; see subjective)

outline – results are supplied by *you* (not provided by Spirit)

perception – a very important concept; perception gives us the
   basis for our reality; a lot of our perceptions are shared with
   others (i.e. mass consciousness)

personal responsibility – it is ultimately true that no-one else
   thinks for you; thereby you create your own reality

physical – includes all that is visible and measurable

Physics – the study of the physical combined with the study of
   matter and energy

      Quantum Physics – the branch of Physics that describes
         physical phenomenon at a scale equivalent to the
         sub-atomic

Planetary model – see electron

Power of Creation – the process by which things move from the invisible to the visible, the non-physical to the physical, or back. Alternatively, it is often known as life itself.

program(med) – the process by which thoughts are implanted into our thinking / behavior; possibly pushed down into our sub-conscious by repetition where said thought rarely has to arrive (back) to a level requiring our attention

    filter – used in conjunction with programming to limit those sensory inputs (or beliefs) available to our consciousness

possibilities – this represents every possible outcome or permutation

prayer – used by religions to effect an affirmation; see affirmation

predict – the supposed ability of science to duplicate an outcome, given certain inputs

probability – see possibilities

rational – the left-brain "thinking" process that uses reason or logic as its basis; see reason

reality – what we see and experience while looking around and moving about; notice the base word: "real"; often used synonymously with Universe

reason – this is attributed to the left-side of the brain; see rational

religion – dominated by the right-brain; earlier religions make their point through stories

responsibility – see personal responsibility

science (scientific) – dominated by logic and reasoning, science produces predictable results

spiritual(ity) – the source of reality; the term is often used by Organized Religion

story(ies) – developed by earlier religions to support right-brain conclusions (via "thinking")

subjective – a term used both in logic and in Religious Science (which refers to the left-brain Finite mind; see objective)

think – the process of consciously engaging left-brain reason, or
    right-brain emotion (with no words involved)
time – this is seen as a base "law" in our reality
        linear –in our reality, time goes in one direction
            only – forward
treatment – Religious Science affirmative prayer that "treats" the
    mind to truth
unity – in mathematics, expressed as the numeral "one" (1); in
    spirituality, everything comes from the same place and is
    related to the same source
Universe – the totality of the non-visible merged with the visible
victim – someone who is subject to their circumstances
visualize – only encompasses left-brain ego and reason; see
    imagination